AFRO-BETS®
Book of Black Heroes
from A to Z

An Introduction to
Important Black Achievers
...ders

...son
...Wesley

The AFRO-BETS Kids™ were created by Wade Hudson and Cheryl Willis Hudson.

Inquiries should be addressed to Just Us Books, P.O. Box 5306, East Orange, NJ 07019
http://justusbooks.com

Library of Congress Card No. 87-82951

ISBN: 978-0-940975-02-6

e-ISBN: 978-0-933491-76-0

Printed in Canada 30 29 28 27 26 25

Foreword to the Revised Edition

AFRO-BETS BOOK OF BLACK HEROES FROM A TO Z was first published in 1988 by Just Us Books. It was the third offering by an independent press determined to produce more books for children and young readers that present the black experience in all of its richness and diversity.

The *AFRO-BETS Book of Black Heroes from A to Z* became an anchor for the fledging company, with hundreds of thousands of copies being sold to schools, libraries, organizations, literacy programs, and parents. It still is the company's top seller.

This popular title also launched a series. *Book of Black Heroes: Great Women in the Struggle* and *Book of Black Heroes: Scientists, Healers and Inventors*, the second and third titles in the Book of Black Heroes series, followed.

The year 2013 marks the 25th anniversary of the release of *AFRO-BETS Book of Black Heroes from A to Z*. We celebrate the occasion with a revised, updated edition of this invaluable resource.

Much has occurred in our nation and around the world during the past 20-plus years. Our country has elected the first African-American president, Barack Obama, who was chosen to serve a second term in office. South African leader Nelson Mandela was not only released from prison, where he had been confined for 27 years, he became the country's first black president. Both leaders have been added to this new edition. Also added are Reverend Vashti Murphy McKenzie, the first African-American woman bishop of the AME Church; Ellen Johnson Sirleaf, president of Liberia, the first black woman to head an African nation in modern times; Jackie Robinson, the first African American to play Major League Baseball in the modern area; and Bishop Richard Allen, one of America's first black leaders.

Many of the original biographies have been expanded and we have changed the format of the pages. The familiar AFRO-BETS Kids graphics have been replaced by sections we call "Did You Know?" and "In His/Her Own Words," both of which add to the depth of information provided on each page. A chronology at the end of the book gives a broad scope of events in black history.

Finally, because January 1, 2013 marked the 150th anniversary of the Emancipation Proclamation, the important decree issued by President Abraham Lincoln that became law on January 1, 1863, we have included a two-page narrative that puts this important step toward African-American freedom in perspective.

This revised edition of *Book of Black Heroes* is also available as an e-book, and in digital format on various tablets and mobile devices.

—*Wade Hudson*

The *AFRO-BETS* *Book of Black Heroes from A to Z*
is dedicated to all those ancestors who helped to pave
the way for a better future for all of us.

CONTENTS

The
Black
Heroes

A

ALDRIDGE, IRA
1805 – 1867

birthplace—New York, NY

"The Man with the Magical Voice"

When Ira was a boy, very few black children dreamed of becoming actors. Black people who lived in the South were still slaves. Those living in northern cities who were free had few opportunities to do what they wanted to do. But Ira was not discouraged. He had a strong, beautiful voice that would someday become famous throughout the world.

Ira attended the African Free School in New York City. Established for the children of free blacks and slaves, it was there that Ira was first introduced to the theater. As a young man, he joined the African Grove Theater, one of the first theaters established by African Americans in the United States. He debuted as Rolla in "Pizzaro" and went on to play Romeo in "Romeo and Juliet" and Hamlet in "Hamlet," both written by William Shakespeare. It was extremely difficult for the African Grove Theater to continue. Many white people didn't want it to succeed. So, in 1824, Ira moved to England to pursue his career in the theater.

For the next 40 years, Ira toured England and other parts of Europe. He performed in many plays and was praised and honored by many kings and princes. His portrayal of Othello in Shakespeare's play made him famous. Ira became one of the best-known actors of his day. But he never returned to the United States. Ira Aldridge is the only black actor among the 33 actors of the British stage honored with bronze plaques at the Shakespeare Memorial Theatre at Stratford-upon-Avon.

Did You Know? The African Grove was founded by William Alexander Brown and James Hewitt. In the beginning, Brown used his backyard as a stage where poetry and short drama pieces were presented. At the suggestion of Hewlett, they hired other black actors and began to stage larger productions. In addition to plays by Shakespeare, the company presented an original work by Brown, "The Drama of King Shotaway," believed to be the first full-length African-American play.

ALI, MUHAMMAD
1942 –

birthplace—Louisville, KY

"The Greatest"

Float like a butterfly, sting like a bee!" Muhammad Ali's trainer yelled to him. Muhammad hit his opponent with three punches and moved quickly away.

"You got him, champ! You got him!" the trainer yelled again. Muhammad landed another punch that knocked out his rival.

"I'm the greatest!" he declared. "I'm the greatest!" Many people agreed with him.

He was born Cassius Clay, but the bold young fighter changed his name when he joined the Nation of Islam. Muhammad showed his winning style inside and outside the ring. Often he predicted the round in which he would win—and he was right most of the time. He first became heavyweight champion of the world in 1964 when he defeated Sonny Liston.

Muhammad refused to join the Army in 1967 during the Vietnam War. He believed war was wrong. Because of this, his boxing title was taken away from him. He was not allowed to box again for nearly four years. But Muhammad gained the respect of many people for standing up for his beliefs. In 1970, he returned to the ring. He defeated George Foreman in 1974 to regain the heavyweight title. In 1978, he lost the title to Leon Spinks but defeated him seven months later, becoming the first fighter to hold the crown three times. Muhammad retired in 1980, as a well-respected champion and humanitarian.

Did You Know? On January 8, 2005, Muhammad Ali was presented the Presidential Citizens Medal and on November 9, 2005, he received the Presidential Medal of Freedom, the highest honor that can be awarded to a civilian by the U.S. government.

ALLEN, RICHARD
1750 – 1831

birthplace—Philadelphia, PA

"The First National Black Leader"

Richard Allen was born into slavery in Philadelphia, PA. When he was a child, he, his parents, and his siblings were sold to a plantation owner in Delaware. When the owner of the plantation ran into financial trouble, he sold Richard's mother and three of her other children.

As Richard grew older he taught himself to read and write and began attending meetings at the local Methodist Society. He became a Methodist, purchased his freedom and began traveling, preaching to both black and white congregants. While in a town near Philadelphia, St. George's Methodist Episcopal Church invited Richard to preach to its African-American members. Allen agreed, although he had to preach at 5:00 a.m. so that the services would not interfere with those for white members. More and more African Americans in the Philadelphia area came to hear Richard's fiery sermons. Concerned about the increasing numbers, officials at St. George's required that African Americans sit in a segregated section. Allen led a walkout in protest.

In 1787, Richard Allen and his friend Absalom Jones formed the Free African Society, where they held their own church services. In 1794, Allen officially established his own church, Bethel, and in 1816, he founded the African Methodist Episcopal church, the first black denomination in the United States. Richard was elected its first bishop. Under Richard's leadership, Bethel became an important stop on the Underground Railroad that helped many enslaved African Americans gain their freedom. Richard Allen was not only a major religious figure; he was one of black America's first national leaders.

Did You Know?	The Free African Society that Richard Allen and Absalom Jones founded was organized like a church. It offered aid to the sick, jobless, orphaned, widowed, and served as an insurance company. It helped newly freed African Americans adjust to freedom. The Free African Society was one of the first black organizations formed in America. Bethel's current church structure, (built 1888–1890) has been designated a national historic landmark.

ANDERSON, MARIAN
1902 – 1993

birthplace—Philadelphia, PA

"A Voice Loved Around the World"

Marian Anderson always loved to sing. When she was six she joined her church choir. Later, she joined other choirs where she continued to develop her singing talent. Church members and friends were so impressed by her talents, they set up a trust fund to help pay for private musical training.

After high school, Marian applied to an all-white music school, the Philadelphia Music Academy, but was turned away because she was black. Undaunted, she continued to take private lessons. Her first big break came when she won first prize in a singing competition sponsored by the New York Philharmonic. As the winner she performed with the orchestra. The successful performance made her a hit with the audience and critics. From there, Marian went on to receive worldwide acclaim during her long career as a concert singer.

In spite of her fame, this talented black woman was denied many opportunities. In 1939, the Daughters of the American Revolution refused to let her perform at Constitution Hall in Washington, DC, Eleanor Roosevelt, President Franklin D. Roosevelt's wife and a member of the organization, resigned in protest. She then arranged for Marian to sing on the steps of the Lincoln Memorial. On Easter morning in 1939, more than 75,000 people came to hear her concert.

Discrimination did not stop Marian. She was the first black person to sing a leading role at the Metropolitan Opera in New York. She sang in countries all over the world and millions of her records have been sold. Marian Anderson retired in 1965.

Did You Know? Although Washington, DC is the nation's capital, for decades segregation was practiced there just as it was in the rest of the country. In 1948, President Harry Truman integrated the U.S. Armed Forces and federal workplaces. Parks and recreation facilities in the United States were integrated in 1954, and public schools were desegregated soon after.

B

BANNEKER, BENJAMIN
1731 – 1806

birthplace—Ellicott, MD

"The Stargazer"

The young man was amazed by the number of stars that appeared in the clear, moonlit sky. "I've never seen so many stars before," he thought. He lay on the ground and began to count them.

This is how Benjamin Banneker spent many of his nights. Neighbors called him "the stargazer."

When Benjamin left school to help on his father's farm, the world became his classroom. He studied the weather, animal life, the stars—everything he could. He read all the books that were available to him. By the time he was 20, Benjamin could answer the most difficult questions in mathematics, science, and philosophy.

In 1761, he carved a wooden clock by hand, using only two models—a pocket watch and an old picture of a clock. It is said that the clock kept nearly perfect time for 50 years.

In 1791, Benjamin was chosen by renowned surveyor Major Andrew Ellicott to help survey federal land where the nation's capital, Washington, DC, would be built. Benjamin provided the astronomical calculations for surveying and the layout of the city. The following year, 1792, Benjamin published the first of a six-year series of almanacs, *Benjamin Banneker's Pennsylvania, Delaware, Maryland and Virginia Almanack and Ephemeris.*

Although Benjamin had never been a slave, he spoke out against the system that held his people in bondage. The young man who studied the stars became an astronomer. But he was also a mathematician, inventor, surveyor, philosopher, and abolitionist.

Did You Know? Benjamin Banneker is often considered the first African-American scientist/inventor. The first African American to receive a patent for an invention, however, was Thomas L. Jennings (1791–1856) for a dry-cleaning process called "dry scouring." Most African Americans, especially those who were slaves, were prohibited from receiving patents until the early twentieth century.

BETHUNE, MARY McLEOD
1875 – 1955

birthplace—Mayesville, SC

"Great Educator"

Mary McLeod Bethune was a determined woman. She helped make education available to thousands of black Americans by starting a school that became Bethune-Cookman University.

When Mary was a child, many people thought that education was a waste of time for black children. But Mary wanted to go to school, and her parents supported her. She graduated from Moody Bible Institute in 1895 and afterward taught school in Georgia. In 1904, she moved to Daytona, FL to establish a school for girls.

Mary had only $1.50 in her pocket when she arrived in Daytona. But that didn't stop her. She sold sweet potato pies to raise money for her school. She asked for donations from churches, clubs, and anyone who would help. Her school became Bethune-Cookman University. It is an example of what a determined person can accomplish.

Mary used that same determination to fight for equal rights for her people. She founded the National Council of Negro Women in 1935. From the 1930s until her death in 1955, she was a leading voice for rights for black Americans. Mary was also an advisor to four presidents of the United States. Her legacy lives on. Mary's home in Daytona Beach is a national historic landmark; her home in Washington, DC in Logan Circle is preserved by the National Park Service as a national historic site and a sculpture of Mary is located in Lincoln Park, in the nation's capital.

" IN HER OWN WORDS "

I leave you love. I leave you hope. I leave you the challenge of developing confidence in one another. I leave you a thirst for education. I leave you a respect for the use of power. I leave you faith. I leave you racial dignity. I leave you a desire to live harmoniously with your fellow men. I leave you, finally, a responsibility to our young people.

—from Mary McLeod Bethune's "Last Will and Testament"

C

CINQUE, JOSEPH
1811 – 1879

birthplace—Sierra Leone, West Africa

"He Would Not Be a Slave"

Joseph Cinque's arms and legs hurt so much he couldn't move them. He and 52 other young Africans were chained together in the bottom of a ship. They had been kidnapped from their village in Sierra Leone, West Africa and taken to Havana, Cuba. Now they were on a ship called the *Amistad*. They were being taken to Principe, Cuba, to work as slaves.

But Joseph was determined to be free. One night, he and the other Africans escaped from their chains. They went to the deck of the ship, seized weapons, and fought the ship's crew. All but two crew members were killed.

"You must return us to our home in Africa," Joseph told the two men. But the men still sailed to the United States. The ship was captured off the coast of Connecticut, and Joseph and the others were arrested.

Abolitionists, who believed slavery was wrong, came to the aid of Joseph and the other Africans. They argued that the Africans were illegally enslaved and were justified in revolting to regain their freedom. After a dramatic appeal before the U.S. Supreme Court led by former president John Quincy Adams in 1841, Joseph and the others were set free.

In 1842, the 35 Africans who had survived their arduous ordeal, including Joseph Cinque, returned to Sierra Leone. They arrived along with five missionaries and teachers who formed a Christian anti-slavery mission in the country.

Did You Know? According to the first census conducted in the United States, in 1790, there were nearly 700,000 blacks held in slavery. By 1860, the year the Civil War began, there were nearly four milllion. From the 16th to the 19th centuries, an estimated 12 to 20 million Africans were shipped as slaves to South America, Central America, and North America. Most of them came from West and Central Africa.

COPPIN, FANNY M.
1836 – 1913

birthplace—Washington, DC

"Dedicated Educator"

Fanny was born a slave in Washington, D.C. When she was 10, her aunt, a free woman, bought Fanny's freedom for $125 and brought her to New Bedford, MA. Later, Fanny moved to Newport, RI, where she worked as a servant, saved her money, took private lessons and went to school. In 1859, she attended the Rhode Island State Normal School. The following year, she entered Oberlin College in Ohio and became the second African-American woman to earn a bachelor's degree. Mary Jane Patterson was the first African-American woman to earn a bachelor's from Oberlin College in 1862.

In 1865, Fanny was chosen to direct the "female department" at the Institute for Colored Youth in Philadelphia, PA. Later to become Cheney State University, the school was founded in 1837 by Quakers.

In 1869, Fanny was appointed principal, becoming the first woman, black or white, to head a coeducational institute in the United States. In her 37 years at the Institute, she advanced the cause of education in Philadelphia and around the country. Coppin State College, an institution of higher learning located in Baltimore, MD, was named in honor of this former slave who became a dedicated educator and leader.

In addition to her career in education, Fanny was also a prominent advocate of women's and African-American rights. In 1897, she was elected vice-president of the National Association of Colored Women, one of the leading organizations of black women at that time.

Did You Know? Cheney State University, considered the first historically black college and university, was established in 1837 in Philadelphia, PA. In 1852, it became one of the first institutions of higher education to train African Americans for skill trades and teaching. Fanny Coppin was the school's principal from 1869 until 1902. She set the tone for its high standards and achievements.

D

DOUGLASS, FREDERICK
1817 – 1895

birthplace—Talbot County, MD

"A Trumpet for Freedom"

As the tall, bearded black man spoke, one could hear a pin drop. When he finished his moving speech, not a dry eye could be found in the entire hall. Many people were troubled to hear about the cruel conditions of slavery. They knew it was bad, but they did not know how often slaves were whipped and killed. Many were surprised to find out that children were taken away from their parents and sold. Frederick Douglass, the greatest anti-slavery speaker of his time, detailed these cruelties and others. Through him, people "experienced" slavery.

Frederick was born a slave in Maryland. He escaped to New York when he was 21 years old. Like many other black people who were able to secure their freedom, he wanted to see the rest of his people free, too.

This self-educated man began to speak out against slavery. Frederick became such a well-known leader that he helped convince President Abraham Lincoln to accept black soldiers into the Union Army. His dynamic speeches attracted many followers in the United States and England.

In 1845, Frederick published his first autobiography, *Narrative of the Life of Frederick Douglass, an American Slave*. Two years later, he established the *North Star* newspaper. He was later named a U.S. marshall in Washington, DC, and in 1889 he was appointed U.S. minister to Haiti.

People are still moved today when they read Frederick Douglass's powerful speeches. He was truly "a trumpet for freedom."

Did You Know? In 1847, Frederick Douglass and several abolitionists friends launched an anti-slavery newspaper called the *North Star.* The name was changed in 1851 to the *Frederick Douglass Papers*, and it continued publication until the 1860s. The first African-American newspaper published in the United States, however, was *Freedom's Journal.* John Russwurm and Samuel Cornish founded it in 1827.

DuBOIS, WILLIAM E.B.
1868 – 1963

birthplace—Great Barrington, MA

"A Gift of Words"

On Tuesday, August 27, 1963, as thousands of people were planning to march on Washington, DC, W.E.B. DuBois died. Some people cried when they heard the news. The great black leader, who had been living in Ghana, West Africa, would be missed.

William was a talented man who was respected throughout the world. He was a scholar, writer, sociologist, philosopher, and leader.

William spent his entire life working for justice and equal rights for black people. He helped organize the National Association for the Advancement of Colored People (NAACP) in 1909. This great civil rights organization has led the fight for black equality for over 100 years. William worked as editor of *Crisis*, the NAACP magazine. He wrote more than 20 books. *Souls of Black Folks* is the best known.

Many people have been involved in the struggle to make a better America. But no one was more outspoken than William. He supported the fight for black rights in Africa and throughout the world, and he was a leader of the peace movement. Not everyone accepted his ideas. He was attacked by those who disagreed with him. After years of struggle in the United States, he moved to Ghana.

On August 28, the historic March on Washington was held. The man with "a gift for words" would have been proud.

" IN HIS OWN WORDS "

Now is the accepted time, not tomorrow, not some more convenient season. It is today that our best work can be done and not some future day or future year. It is today that we fit ourselves for the greater usefulness of tomorrow. Today is the seed time, now are the hours of work, and tomorrow comes the harvest and the playtime.
                                                                    —William E.B. DuBois

DuSABLE, JEAN BAPTISTE
1745 – 1818

birthplace—Haiti

"Founder of Chicago"

Chicago, IL, is one of the largest cities in the United States. But few people know it was founded by a black man, Jean DuSable.

Jean was born in Haiti, the world's oldest black republic. He moved to St. Louis, MO, where he became a fur trader. When the British took over St. Louis, Jean moved to Peoria, IL, where Native Americans helped him establish a successful trading business.

Jean made many trips to Canada to bring back furs. He always passed a place called Eschikagov that he used as a lookout point. In 1774, he built a cabin there for his family. Other pioneers built stores and homes near his post. The settlement grew into a city that became Chicago.

Many years passed before Jean was credited with the founding of Chicago. For a long time the city did not honor Jean as it had honored other pioneers. In 1912, the city of Chicago commemorated Jean's homestead with a plaque on the corner of Kinzie and Pine Streets. African-American groups campaigned for Jean to be honored at the 1933–34 Century of Progress International Exposition held in Chicago. At the time, few had even heard of Jean DuSable. The campaign was successful and a replica of Jean's cabin was presented as part of the "background of the history of Chicago." Then, on May 11, 1976, the Jean Baptiste Point Du Sable Homesite was designated as a National Historic Landmark.

Did You Know? When Jean Baptiste DuSable sold his trading post in 1800 to John Kinzie, who was acting on the behalf of Jean La Lime, it included a house, two barns, a horse-drawn mill, a bakehouse, a poultry house, a dairy, and a smokehouse. In 1913, a historical librarian with the State Historical Society of Wisconsin discovered the bill of sale from Jean du Sable to Jean La Lime in an archive in Detroit. This document outlined all of the property Jean owned as well as many of his personal artifacts. The city of Chicago was incorporated on Saturday, March 4, 1837. It has the third largest African-American population in the United States.

DUNHAM, KATHERINE
1910 – 2006

birthplace—Joliet, IL

"Pioneer of Black Dance"

Katherine Dunham performs "L'Aq Ya," an early creation based on a Martinique fighting dance.

Katherine Dunham was a dancer, choreographer, and anthropologist. She used her many talents to make an important gift to the world.

When Katherine was a college student, she won a scholarship to study anthropology in Haiti. While she was there, she studied Haitian dances. Katherine was the first person to realize how important these dances were. She believed they could teach people many things about black history and culture. She knew they should be shared with the world.

When Katherine returned to the United States, she brought the dances with her. She formed a company of black dancers that became famous throughout the world.

Katherine blended African and Caribbean dance styles with modern dance. These dance styles highlighted more flexible movements of the body. When integrated with techniques of ballet and traditional modern dance, a new form of modern dance emerged—Black Dance. Katherine was known as one of the pioneers of this new dance style.

Katherine traveled to many nations and studied the dances of many cultures. She used the beautiful language of dance to teach people about themselves and others. Many of the dances she created are still being performed today. Her most popular works include "Afrique du Nord," "Southland," "Blues Trio," and "Veracuzana."

Did You Know? In 1945, Katherine Dunham opened and directed the Katherine Dunham School of Dance and Theatre in New York City. Among those who attended classes at the school were Warren Beatty, James Dean, José Ferrer, Jennifer Jones, Eartha Kitt, Shirley McLaine, Gregory Peck, Sidney Poitier, and Shelley Winters.

E

ELLINGTON, DUKE
1899 – 1974

birthplace—Washington, DC

"Take the A Train"

Duke Ellington (born Edward Kennedy Ellington) was a great conductor and composer. His special style of music made his famous around the world. He created jazz songs and orchestra music that influenced many musicians and attracted millions of fans. Duke was born and grew up in Washington, D.C. Both his father and mother were pianists. As a youngster, Duke showed talent as a pianist. He didn't like to practice, but he practiced anyway. His friends began to call him "Duke" because he liked to dress in fancy clothes.

Music became Duke's full-time job when he was 18. He formed his own band, which performed in Washington, D.C. In 1923, he moved to New York City. There, he became a major figure of the Harlem Renaissance and one of the most important music performers and composers in the country.

Duke's career spanned more than 50 years. His broad approach to music included Blues, Gospel, Pop and classical. He composed for films and stage musicals. Duke received many awards, and played for kings, queens, and presidents of the United States.

He wrote over 1,000 songs and performed in nightclubs and concert halls around the world. Many of the world's most outstanding musicians have been influenced by the Duke and his music. "Take the A Train" and "Sophisticated Lady" are just two songs made popular by Duke Ellington.

Did You Know? Ragtime and Blues, two earlier African-American music styles, were important influences on the early development of Jazz. Ragtime reached its peak popularity between 1897 and 1918. Blues emerged in the Southern part of the United States during the early 1890s. Jazz began in the early 1900s, and by 1920s, it had become one of America's most popular music forms.

F

FRANKLIN, ARETHA
1942 –

birthplace—Memphis, TN

"Queen of Soul"

R-E-S-P E-C T. Respect. That word was very important to black people, particularly in the 1960s. Aretha Franklin, who sang about it, earned the respect of everyone who heard her.

Beautiful black voices were always part of Aretha's life. Her father was a well-known preacher. Famous black singers like Dinah Washington, Mahalia Jackson, and B.B. King often visited her home. Music was important to Aretha's family, and it would be a very important part of Aretha's life, too.

When Aretha was 12, she made her first record. By the time she graduated from high school, she knew that she wanted to be a professional singer. At first, she sang only Gospel songs. But later she began to sing popular music. Soon, everyone was singing her songs and everyone knew who she was. In 1967, she recorded a number of chart-topping songs. Aretha Franklin became known as the "Queen of Soul." Ever since then, she has been one of the best-known singers in the United States.

Aretha Franklin has won 18 Grammy Awards and holds the record for most Best Female R&B Vocal Performance awards, with eleven honors in that category. In 2005, she was awarded the Presidential Medal of Freedom, and in 2009, she sang at the inauguration ceremonies for President Barack Obama.

Did You Know? Soul music began in the mid 1950s when performers like Ray Charles mixed elements of Rhythm & Blues with Gospel music. By the 1960s, Soul was the most popular music in African-American communities. In 1967, Aretha Franklin recorded "I Never Loved a Man (The Way I Love You)," launching her career as a Soul singer.

G

GARVEY, MARCUS
1887 – 1940

birthplace—Jamaica

"Back to Africa"

It was one of the most splendid parades ever. Trumpets blasted and drums beat. More than 50,000 people sang proud songs and said proud words. At the head of the parade marched Marcus Garvey in a uniform of purple and gold.

Marcus and the thousands of black people who marched with him were proud of their African heritage. They believed that Africa was a great continent and that Africans were a great people. They were determined to help Africa regain its place in history.

Marcus was born in Jamaica. In 1916, he came to the United States and established the Universal Negro Improvement Association (UNIA), an organization that he had founded in Jamaica. He planned to build black pride in the United States by encouraging black people to build a black nation in Africa. His movement was called the "Back to Africa" movement.

Marcus set up grocery stores, restaurants, and a newspaper. He also established The Black Star Line, a fleet of steamships that would return people to their homeland. Thousands of people sent him money. In 1925, the U.S. government accused Marcus of using the mail to cheat his supporters. He was put in jail, and his ships never sailed.

Although his dream failed, Marcus helped his people develop new feelings of hope and self-respect. He taught black people that they could do great things if they believed in themselves and worked together. That is why many people call him a hero today.

Did You Know? More than a hundred years before Marcus Garvey, Paul Cuffe believed that Africa was a good place for African Americans to go to escape slavery in the United States. In 1815, he used his ship to take 38 African Americans and a cargo of goods to Sierra Leone, West Africa. Although he was unable to make another trip, he continued to be a part of the back-to-Africa movement of the early 1800s.

GIBSON, ALTHEA
1927 – 2003

birthplace—Silver, NC

"She Kept Her Eye the Ball"

Tennis is a very exciting sport. But very few black people were recognized as great tennis players before Althea Gibson came along. Althea grew up in New York City. There were very few tennis courts in her neighborhood, but Althea was determined to learn the game and become successful.

In 1946 she moved to Wilmington, NC, to work on her tennis game with Dr. Hubert A. Eaton. Then she went to Florida A&M University, where she graduated in 1953.

Althea won a number of singles titles of the American Tennis Association, an African-American organization established to promote and sponsor tennis tournaments for black players. But she was not allowed to play in the world's best tournament. Finally, in 1951, after an article written by former tennis star Alice Mable lambasting her sport for its discrimination, Althea was allowed to play at Wimbledon. In 1957 and 1958, she won championships at Wimbledon, and at the U.S. Open in Forest Hills, New York. She was also ranked number one in the world among women players in 1957 and 1958. She became the first black person to compete in the U.S. National Championship and the first to win major titles in tennis.

Sometimes called the "Jackie Robinson of tennis," Althea Gibson became an international tennis star and an inspiration to others.

Did You Know? Arthur Ashe was the first African-American male tennis champion. He won the 1968 U.S. Open, the 1970 Australian Open, and the 1975 Wimbledon championship. During the first decade of the 21st century, women's tennis was dominated by the Williams sisters—Venus and Serena. Between them, the two sisters have won more than 100 singles and doubles titles.

HANSBERRY, LORRAINE
1930 – 1965

birthplace—Chicago, IL

"Young, Gifted and Black"

I care. I admit it. I care about it all. It takes too much energy not to care!
— from "To Be Young, Gifted and Black," Act II

When Lorraine Hansberry was a girl, her family moved to a white neighborhood. It was during a time when black and white people usually lived in separate parts of town. Many of their neighbors were angry that the Hansberry family had moved into a white section of town. When Lorraine walked to school, many people called her names and made fun of her. She was very frightened.

Lorraine never forgot how hard her family had fought against discrimination. That served as inspiration for her famous play, *A Raisin in the Sun* about a black family that wants to move into a white neighborhood. It is also about the love, pride, and strength that holds many black families together. *A Raisin in the Sun* was the first play by a black woman to be produced on Broadway.

Lorraine died at an early age, but many people consider her to be one of America's finest playwrights.

Did You Know? When *A Raisin in the Sun* opened in 1959, it was also the first play on Broadway to be directed by an African American—Lloyd Richards. The cast was comprised some of the country's best black actors and actresses, including Ruby Dee, Ivan Dixon, Lonne Elder III, Louis Gossett, Jr., Claudia McNeil, Sidney Poitier, Diane Sands, Glynn Turman, and Douglas Turner Ward.

HENSON, MATTHEW
1902 – 1993

birthplace—Charles County, MD

"A Great Explorer"

In 1918, Matthew Henson, Robert Peary and 22 men in their party left New York City headed for the northern most part of the earth. There, they planned to become the first men to reach the North Pole. Peary and Henson, who was one of his most important assistants, had tried before. But the frigid weather and rough terrain stopped them. This time, they were determined to reach their goal.

On April 6, 1909, the two explorers, along with four Inuit guides, Ootah, Seegloo, Eqiqingwah and Ooquash, were only a few miles from their greatest triumph. The rest of the party had stayed behind. Peary, however, became very ill. So Matthew continued. A short time later, Matthew Henson placed the U.S. flag at the North Pole, becoming the first person in history to achieve this monumental feat. Although some have disputed this claim, it is now gerpeally accepted that Matthew Henson, Robert Perry, and their four guides were the first to reach the North Pole.

Matthew was 21 when he met Admiral Peary. They made many trips together. During the Admiral's expeditions to the North Pole, Matthew played an important role. He spoke the language of the Eskimos, built sleds, and trained teams of dogs. He solved many problems and gave valuable advice.

Nearly 81 years went by before the accomplishments of this great explorer were fully recognized. On April 6, 1988, Matthew's remains were reburied with full military honors at Arlington National Cemetery in Washington, D.C.

Did You Know? Sophia Danenberg (born 1972) was the first African American and the first black woman to climb to the summit of Mount Everest in the Himalayas mountain range of South Asia. Withstanding bad weather, and suffering from bronchitis and congestion, Danenberg reached the top of the world's tallest mountain on May 19, 2006.

HUGHES, LANGSTON
1902 – 1967

birthplace—Joplin, MO

"A Pen for a Sword"

I've known rivers:
I've known rivers ancient as the world and older than the
flow of human blood in human veins.
My soul has grown deep like rivers.
                    — from "The Negro Speaks of Rivers"

No one enjoyed writing more than Langston Hughes. He was a poet, but he also wrote plays, songs, newspaper articles, and books.

Langston wrote about the lives and conditions of black Americans. People enjoyed his warm and humorous style. He had a gift for making others understand how black people lived, worked, talked, and played.

Langston's first poem was published when he was 19. That poem, "The Negro Speaks of Rivers" is still one of his most popular works.

The Harlem Renaissance in the 1920s and 1930s was an important era for black writers and artists. Langston was one of the most important writers of that period.

Langston published ten volumes of poetry and numerous short stories and anthologies. He also produced plays and operas. He was recognized throughout the world as one of America's finest writers.

In 1960, the NAACP presented Langston with the Spingarn Medal, declaring him "Poet Laureate of the Negro Race." He continued to write and travel until his death in 1967.

Did You Know? Langston Hughes was one of the most versatile writers in the United States. He wrote novels, short stories, plays, poetry, operas, essays, and works for children. His ashes are interred in the Schomburg Center for Research in Black Culture in Harlem beneath a floor medallion in the middle of the foyer leading to the auditorium named for him. The design on the floor covering his remains is an cosmogram titled "Rivers." The title is taken from Hughes' poem, "The Negro Speaks of Rivers."

HURSTON, ZORA NEALE
1903 – 1960

birthplace—Eatonville, FL

"A Southern Genius"

Here is peace. She pulled in her horizon like a giant fish-net. Pulled it around the waist of the world and draped it over her shoulder. So much of life in its meshes. She called in her soul to come and see!
—from *Their Eyes Were Watching God*

Zora was a bright little girl with a mischievous spirit. Her father warned that her curiosity would get her in trouble—that "the white folks wouldn't stand for it." But her mother told her to "jump at the sun," and that is just what Zora did.

Zora was born in Eatonville, a self-governing black town in Florida. She loved to listen to stories on the back porch of the general store where people in her town gathered. It was there that Zora developed a love for language and folktales.

Zora was a writer, but she also studied and collected folktales. She celebrated the lives of black people in her novels and folktale collections. She followed her mother's advice. Zora was never afraid to express her feelings or live the way she wanted to live. Writers admire her unique gift of telling stories in the wonderful style that captures everyday life. Zora's published work included short stories, poems, anthologies, and novels. Her most popular novel is *Their Eyes Were Watching God*.

Did You Know? For many years, Zora Neale Hurston's contributions to literature went unrecognized. In 1975, writer Alice Walker wrote an article in *Ms.* magazine titled "In Search of Zora Neale Hurston." It revived interest in Hurston and her work. Today, Hurston's novels and poetry are studied in literature classes, women's studies and black studies courses, and are popular with the general reading public.

INGRAM, REX
1895 – 1969

birthplace—riverboat on
the Mississippi

"A Dynamic Actor"

Rex Ingram was one of America's most talented actors. He appeared in movies and stage productions that were enjoyed by Americans everywhere.

Rex was born aboard a riverboat where his father worked. He became interested in acting when he attended military school. In 1919, he began his acting career with a role in the first *Tarzan* movie. Afterwards, he was featured in such films as *Lord Jim*, *Beau Geste*, *King Kong*, *Green Pastures*, and *Huckleberry Finn*.

Although Rex was an excellent actor, he was denied many roles because of his color. But he loved to act and didn't get discouraged.

Rex was one of the few black actors to serve on the board of directors of the Studio Actor's Guild, the famous actors' union. Throughout his career, he fought to open doors for other African Americans in the movie industry.

One of Rex's best known roles was in *Cabin in the Sky*, in which he played Lucifer, Jr. This famous movie, released in 1943, had an all-black cast that featured some of the finest performers of the time, including Lena Horne, Ethel Waters, and Eddie "Rochester" Anderson.

In 1962, Rex became the first African-American actor to be hired for a contract role on a soap opera, when he appeared on *The Brighter Day*.

Did You Know? Rex Ingram and other black actors faced discrimination throughout their careers in the movie industry. One African American set out to do something about their difficult plight. From 1919 to 1948, Oscar Micheaux wrote, produced, and directed 44 feature-length films that featured black performers. Called the "Father of Black Film," Oscar first introduced Paul Robeson to the movie-going public in a 1924 film titled *Body and Soul*.

JACKSON, JESSE
1941 –

birthplace—Greenville, SC

"The Country Preacher"

"Ladies and gentlemen," said the announcer. "I would like to introduce the man who will be the 1984 Democratic nominee for President of the United States—Reverend Jesse Jackson!" Everyone clapped and cheered. Jesse proudly stepped to the front of the platform. He raised his arms and gave the "V" sign for victory.

In 1984, Jesse Jackson became the first black man to seek the presidential nomination of a major political party. Few people in Jesse's hometown could have imagined how important he would become. When he was young, many children teased him because his mother wasn't married when he was born. But Jesse always knew he was a special person. He was determined to succeed. He was an outstanding football player and school leader in high school. He also excelled in college activities at North Carolina A & T.

During the 1960s, Jesse joined the civil rights movement. He became a member of the Southern Christian Leadership Conference (SCLC), and worked closely with Dr. Martin Luther King, Jr. In 1967, he gained wide power and respect when he was appointed director of Operation Breadbasket, a program that helped people in large cities obtain jobs and housing. A year later, Jesse became a minister.

In 1971, he organized Operation PUSH (People United to Save Humanity). This organization is still fighting for equality for all.

In 1988, Jesse ran an even stronger campaign to gain the Democratic nomination for president. He won a number of states and finished second in many others. Some people were surprised by the support he received. Although he did not win, Jesse Jackson rose from a humble beginning to become a very influential man in America. His efforts in the political arena help set the stage for the election of the first black president of the United States, Barack Obama.

Did You Know? In 1848, abolitionist Frederick Douglass became the first African American to receive a vote for the office of president of the United States at a national political convention. Others to receive more than one vote at a national convention include Channing E. Phillips in 1968 (67.5 votes), Shirley Chisholm, 1972 (152 votes), Jesse Jackson, 1984 (466 votes), Jesse Jackson, 1988 (1218.5 votes), and Alan Keyes, 2000 (6 votes).

JOHNSON, JAMES WELDON
1871 – 1938

birthplace—Jacksonville, FL

"A Way with Words"

Lift every voice and sing,
'til earth and heaven ring—
Ring with the harmonies of liberty

These were beautiful words that would be sung long after James Weldon Johnson wrote them. In 1900, James penned this verse to music composed by his brother, John. Their song "Lift Every Voice and Sing" became known as the Negro national anthem. Generations of black people have sung their song with pride.

James was an educator, poet, novelist, diplomat, and civil rights leader. He cared deeply about his people and worked to improve their lives. Black culture was important to James. He wrote many important books about black people's contributions to music, religion, and theater. He also wrote a novel called *The Autobiography of an Ex-Colored Man*. In 1920, he became the executive secretary of the NAACP, a position he held for ten years.

James also served as a diplomat and consul for the United States in Venezuela and Nicaragua.

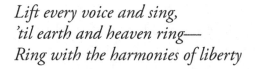

Did You Know? James Weldon Johnson was the first African American to serve as executive director of the NAACP. Founded in 1909, it is the oldest civil rights organization in the United States. James served as executive director from 1920 to 1931. He was succeeded by Walter White (1931–1955), Roy Wilkins (1955–1977), Benjamin Hooks (1977–1992), Benjamin Chavis (1993–1994), Kweisi Mfume (1996–2004), and Benjamin Todd Jealous (2008–present).

KAY, ULYSSES
1917 – 1995

birthplace—Tucson, AZ

"A Classical Giant"

Some people believed that classical, western music was too difficult for black people to master. Men like William Grant Still, Dean Dixon, and Ulysses Kay proved them wrong. These talented black men became outstanding composers and conductors.

Ulysses Kay decided to make music his career when he was young. He had always loved music, but he knew he had to study hard if he wanted to succeed. He attended the Eastman School of Music, the Berkshire Music Center, and Yale University. He learned to "compose" or write music.

After serving in the U.S. Navy during World War II, Ulysses quickly became the most important black composer of classical music in the United States. He received numerous awards, including the Gershwin Memorial Prize, a Broadcast Music, Inc. award, and an American Broadcasting Company prize.

He wrote five operas, including *Oboe Concerto* (1940), *A Short Overture* (1947), and *The Juggler of Our Lady* (1962), three of his most popular works.

Ulysses Kay will be remembered not only as a great composer, but also as a black pioneer in classical, western music.

Did You Know? Harry T. Burleigh (1866–1948) was another distinguished African-American composer, arranger, and professional singer. He helped to make black music available to classically trained artists by introducing them to the music and by arranging the music, particularly Spirituals, in a more classical form.

KING, MARTIN LUTHER, JR.
1929 – 1968

birthplace—Atlanta, GA

"Drum Major for Justice"

It was 1955. A group of black people gathered in a local church in Montgomery, AL. Many were angry because Rosa Parks had been arrested for refusing to give her bus seat to a white man. They wanted to do something about the discrimination they had faced in Montgomery. A young minister was chosen as their leader. His name was Martin Luther King, Jr.

Martin was the son of a minister. So, many people assumed he would become a minister, too.

Young Martin was an excellent student. He studied hard, but he enjoyed it because he loved to learn. In 1948, Martin graduated from Morehouse College. He was only 19. Three years later, he received a bachelor of divinity degree from Crozer Theological Seminary. Boston University awarded him a doctorate degree in 1955.

Martin was 25 when he was chosen to become pastor of the Dexter Avenue Baptist Church in Montgomery. He quickly impressed church members with his speaking and organizing abilities. His stirring sermons drew people from all over the city.

Many of the people assembled in this Montgomery church in 1955 knew this was the man to lead them.

The bus boycott that Martin led ended segregated seating on Montgomery public buses. But he did not stop there. Martin headed a long struggle for equal justice in America. A few decades ago, in many American cities, black people could not vote. They could not drink from the same water fountain or use the same restroom as white people. Black children could not go to the same schools that white children attended. Martin helped to end these injustices.

The struggle to end these injustices wasn't easy. Thousands of people went to jail, were beaten, and killed. But Martin didn't believe in violence. He used peaceful methods of protest, such as sit-ins, marches, and boycotts.

In 1963, Martin led the historic March on Washington, where he gave his famous "I Have a Dream" speech. A year later he was awarded the Nobel Peace Prize. Years later, in 1986, a national holiday was declared to honor this great American. The people assembled in 1955 couldn't have known how great Martin would become.

Dr. Martin Luther King, Jr. was assassinated in Memphis, Tennessee on April 4, 1968 by James Earl Ray. He was only 39 years old, but he did as much as anyone could to secure equality and justice for all Americans.

Did You Know? In 1983, the third Monday of January of each year was declared a national holiday in honor of Dr. Martin Luther King, Jr. It was first observed in 1986, although some states refused to recognize the holiday. It wasn't until the year 2000 that all 50 states officially observed Dr. Martin Luther King, Jr. Day. On August 22, 2011, the Dr. Martin Luther King, Jr. Memorial opened in Washington, D.C. to the public. Covering four acres, the memorial includes the "Stone of Hope," a 30-foot statue of Dr. King, and a 450-foot inscription wall made from granite panels that is inscribed with 14 excerpts from Dr. King's sermons and public speeches. It is the first major memorial along the National Mall to be dedicated to an African American.

L

LEWIS, EDMONIA
1845 – 1907

birthplace—near Albany, NY

"She Made Stone 'Talk' "

Edmonia Lewis was such a talented sculptor, she seemed to make stones "talk." Her sculptures tell a story. One of her most famous works, a marble sculpture called "Forever Free," is a study of a black man greeting freedom at the end of the Civil War. One of his hands is clenched in a fist, the other protects his wife. Many people believe that this sculpture captures the two strong feelings that many black people felt when they were declared free from slavery—joy in their freedom and fear that it would be taken away. Edmonia also created busts of famous people who fought to end slavery. Her busts of John Brown, Charles Sumner, and William Story captured the spirit and determination that made these men strong fighters for justice.

Edmonia's father was a black American and her mother was a Native American. Named Mary Edmonia Lewis at birth, she was one of the first women to attend Oberlin College where she began her studies in fine art. After leaving Oberlin in 1862, Edmonia moved to Boston in 1863 and further developed her artistic talent by studying with a well-known sculptor, Edward Augustus Brackett. Later she went to Rome, Italy, where she set up a studio within the former studio of Italian sculptor Antonio Canova. In Italy, Edmonia embraced a neoclassical style, had frequent exhibitions, and became very popular. She later exhibited one of her most powerful works, "The Death of Cleopatra" at the 1876 Centennial Exposition in Philadelphia.

Edmonia was also a fighter for freedom. She was involved in the Underground Railroad that made it possible for slaves to escape to the North. She also helped organize one of the first black regiments to fight in the Civil War. Edmonia Lewis was one of the first black Americans to be recognized as a great artist.

Did You Know? Henry Ossawa Tanner (1859–1937) was an African-American painter who was born 14 years after Edmonia Lewis. Like Edmonia, Henry moved to Europe because there were greater opportunities there for black Americans. Whereas Edmonia went to Italy, Henry chose Paris, France. He was the first African-American painter to achieve international success. The "Banjo Lesson" is his most well-known painting.

LOCKE, ALAIN
1886 – 1954

birthplace—Philadelphia, PA

"A Black Intellectual"

It must be increasingly recognized that the Negro has already made very substantial contributions, not only in his folk-art and music especially which has already found appreciation, but in larger, though humbler and less acknowledged ways.

— from Alain Locke's *The New Negro*

Alain Locke enjoyed helping people. It made him feel good to help others succeed. He especially liked to help those who were creative. Many aspiring writers and artists looked to him for encouragement and assistance.

Alain was an educator, writer, historian, and critic. He wrote many books and articles that helped people understand the contributions black Americans made to American culture.

In 1907, he graduated from Howard University and became the first black person selected as a Rhodes Scholar, an academic honor and scholarship awarded to only a few outstanding students each year.

Alain was one of the leaders of the Harlem Renaissance of the 1920s and 1930s. At first, people recognized only black writers. Alain helped make them aware of black artists and musicians, too.

For 36 years he taught at Howard University. Alain was one of America's brightest scholars.

Did You Know? Alain Locke encouraged black American artists, writers, and musicians to look to Africa as an inspiration for their works. He said they should depict African and African-American life and draw from their own history for subject material.

MANDELA, NELSON
1918 – 2013

birthplace—Mvezo, South Africa

"African Freedom Fighter"

Rolihlahla Mandela was the first member of his family to attend a school. There his teacher gave him the English name "Nelson." Mandela continued his education at the University College of Fort Hare and the University of Witwatersrand and in 1942, he was qualified in law. In 1944, he joined the African National Congress, an organization formed to increase the rights of Black South Africans.

In 1960, the South African government banned the ANC, rendering activities by activists like Mandela illegal. In 1963, Mandela was arrested and after a trial was sentenced to life imprisonment. From 1964 to 1982, Nelson Mandela was imprisoned at Robben Island. Later he was sent to Pollsmoor Prison, where he served the remainder of his sentence.

During his years in prison, Nelson Mandela's reputation grew. He was widely recognized as the most important black leader in South Africa. He consistently refused to compromise his political position to obtain his freedom and became a symbol of the resistance against apartheid.

On February 11, 1990, after international pressure on the government of South Africa, Mandela was released from prison. In 1991, the South African government repealed apartheid laws and on April 27, 1994, the first democratically held elections took place. Mandela was elected the country's first black president.

Nelson Mandela is also widely recognized as a world leader and man of peace. In November 2009, the United Nations General Assembly declared July 18 "Nelson Mandela Day" to mark his contribution to world freedom.

Did You Know? Bishop Desmond Tutu is another world leader from South Africa. A bishop in the Anglican Church, he fought to end apartheid in his country and has been vocal in support of human rights and the plight of the poor and oppressed. He has received many awards for his work, including the Nobel Peace Prize, (1984); the Albert Schweitzer Prize for Humanitarianism, (1986); the Mahatma Ghandi Prize, (2005), and the Presidential Medal of Freedom (2009).

MARSHALL, THURGOOD
1908 – 1993

birthplace—Baltimore, MD

"Supreme Court Justice"

Thurgood Marshall always cared about his fellow man. When he practiced law in Baltimore, MD, he represented many clients without getting paid.

Thurgood graduated with honors from Howard University Law School. In 1940, he was named chief counsel for the National Association for the Advancement of Colored People. During his years with the NAACP, Thurgood and his staff won 29 out of 32 Supreme Court cases. His most famous victory came in the 1954 *Brown vs. Board of Education* of Topeka, Kansas case. This historic decision overturned the "separate but equal" doctrine that had justified segregation since 1896.

In 1965, Thurgood was appointed solicitor general of the United States. When a vacancy occurred on the Supreme Court, President Lyndon Johnson nominated Thurgood for the seat. In 1967, this great jurist became the first black justice of the U.S. Supreme Court. Thurgood served on the Supreme Court for 24 years, compiling a record that included strong support for Constitutional protection of individual rights, especially the rights of criminal suspects against the government and civil rights. Marshall dedicated his life to protecting the rights of all Americans and on the occasion of the bicentennial of the U.S. Constitution he wrote:

"Some may more quietly commemorate the suffering, struggle, and sacrifice that has triumphed over much of what was wrong with the original document, and observe the anniversary with hopes not realized and promises not fulfilled. I plan to celebrate the bicentennial of the Constitution as a living document, including the Bill of Rights and the other amendments protecting individual freedoms and human rights."

Did You Know? In his dual role as a Howard University law professor and NAACP special counsel, Charles Hamilton Houston (b. 1895–d. 1950) played a major role in the struggle to end legal racial discrimination in the United States. He helped train Thurgood Marshall and many other prominent African-American lawyers during his tenure at Howard. Because of his courtroom successes fighting discrimination, he became known as "The Man Who Killed Jim Crow."

MAYS, WILLIE
1931 –

birthplace—Westfield, AL

"Say, Hey!"

Willie ran fast. He hit like a champ. He slugged 660 home runs. For over 20 years, this great player proved he could do it all. He was one of the most exciting men to ever play professional baseball.

Willie started his professional baseball career in 1947 with the Chattanooga Shoo-Shoos, an all-black team. Then he joined the Birmingham Black Barons of the Negro American League. Because Major League Baseball was segregated, African Americans formed their own leagues and teams. The first professional Negro baseball league, the Negro National League, was formed in 1920 by Rube Walker. The year Willie started his baseball career, 1947, was the same year that Jackie Robinson broke the color barrier in Major League Baseball.

The New York Giants bought Willie's contract from the Birmingham Black Barons in 1950. He was sent to a minor league team to gain experience. But Willie played so well, the Giants soon invited him to join their team. On May 24, 1951, Willie made his major league debut. He had a rocky beginning. It took 13 times at bats before he got his first hit. After that, Willie became a sensation. He went on to win the 1951 Rookie of the Year award, which honors the best new player of the season.

Willie usually greeted people by saying "Say, Hey." He became known as the "Say, Hey Kid." After a long, successful career with the Giants and the New York Mets, Willie was elected to the Baseball Hall of Fame in 1979.

Did You Know? Many people know that Jackie Robinson was the first African American to play Major League Baseball in the modern era. Most don't know, however, that later that year, 1947, Larry Doby (1932–1993) became the first African American to play for an American League team when he suited up for the Cleveland Indians. The Brooklyn Dodgers, the team for which Robinson played, was in the National League. Unfortunately, many of the stars of the Negro Baseball Leagues never got a chance to display their skills in the major leagues.

McKENZIE, VASHTI
1947 –

birthplace—Augusta, GA

"First Female AME Bishop"

Vashti McKenzie was born into a prominent African-American family. In 1892, her great grandfather, John H. Murphy, started the *Afro-American* newspaper in Baltimore, MD. Her grandmother was a founding member of Delta Sigma Theta, a national sorority.

Vashti attended Morgan State University, but left school to marry Stan McKenzie, her college sweetheart. Stan went on to play professional basketball. After he retired, the couple moved back to Baltimore, where Vashti continued her education and received a bachelor's degree in journalism from the University of Maryland.

After graduating she joined the staff at her family's newspaper, hosted a television show and worked for two local Gospel radio stations. Then she joined Bethel AME Church in Baltimore, where she visited the sick and assisted in promoting church activities through the media.

In her late 30s, McKenzie entered Howard University School of Divinity where she received a master's degree in Theology. She later earned a Doctor of Ministry degree from United Theological Seminary in Dayton, OH.

After receiving her divinity degree from Howard, Vashti was assigned to a small church in Chesapeake City, MD. In 1990, she became the first female pastor of Payne Memorial AME Church in Baltimore. Ten years later, Vashti McKenzie made history when she was elected the first female bishop of the AME church.

Did You Know? Like the AME Church, the African Methodist Episcopal Zion Church has roots in the white Methodist Episcopal Church. Following discrimination at the John Street Methodist Church in New York City, many black worshippers left and in 1800, built their own church. Other black congregations followed the model. At first, only white ministers were allowed to pastor these churches. Then, in 1820, six AME Zion churches selected James Varick as their first general superintendent. In 1822, he was ordained as the first bishop of the AME Zion church.

MOTLEY, CONSTANCE B.
1921 – 2005

birthplace—New Haven, CT

"Woman of Distinction"

Constance Baker Motley was born in the small state of Connecticut. But the legal battles she won made a big difference in the lives of her people.

As a lawyer, Constance fought many important civil rights' battles. One of her most famous victories gave James Meredith the right to become a student at the University of Mississippi. During the 1950s, it was against the law for black and white students in the South to attend college together. Constance fought for James Meredith's right to attend the school of his choice. Her victory struck an important blow against segregation in southern universities. James Meredith was admitted to the University of Mississippi in 1962.

In 1965, Constance was elected Manhattan borough president in New York City. She was the first black person and first woman to hold that powerful office. One year later, President Lyndon Johnson appointed her a U.S. district judge. Constance Baker Motley helped prove that the courts and law are powerful weapons in the fight for justice. She was honored for her important contributions with induction into the national Women's Hall of Fame and posthumously with the Presidential Citizens Medal, awarded by former President Bill Clinton in 2011.

Did You Know? Charlotte E. Ray (1850–1911) was the first African-American woman lawyer in the United States. She was also the first woman to graduate from the Howard University School of Law (1872). She was admitted to the District of Columbia Bar in 1872 and soon after opened a law office in the nation's capital. Because of racial and gender discrimination, she was forced to close her office. She later moved to New York City where she taught in the public school system.

NKRUMAH, KWAME
1909 – 1972

birthplace—Ghana, West Africa

"Africa Must Unite"

The African continent had many strong and powerful nation-states. But beginning in the 15th century, Dutch, French, and other Europeans took over many of them. For more than 400 years, many Africans were forced to live under foreign rule. Throughout the continent, people were denied rights as citizens in their own land.

Kwame Nkrumah spent most of his life fighting to bring independence to his country. Born in the western province of the Gold Coast, Kwame was educated in the United States and England. He was active in organizations that fought for reform in his country. He became prime minister in 1952. In 1957, the Gold Coast became the first black nation in Africa to regain its independence. Ghana was chosen as its official name. Kwame Nkrumah became president in 1960.

Other African nations looked to Kwame for guidance in their struggle for independence. They knew he believed, "Africa must unite."

Kwame was a founding member of the Organization of African Unity, an organization established in 1963 to promote unity among African nations. The name was changed to the African Union in 2002.

Did You Know? During the late 1950 and 1960s, many countries in Africa gained their independence. Many heads of those countries emerged as international leaders in the struggle for black equality around the world. In addition to Kwame Nkrumah, African leaders included Sekou Toure (Guinea), Leopold Senghor (Senegal), Julius Nyerere (Tanzania), Jomo Kenyatta (Kenya), and Milton Obote (Uganda).

O

OBAMA, BARACK HUSSEIN
1961 –

birthplace—Honolulu, HI

"First African-American President of the United States"

A crowd of nearly a quarter-million people filled Grant Park in Chicago, IL, on the evening of November 4, 2008. They were people of all races and ethnicities. They were young and old, rich and poor, students, and senior citizens. They were all gathered there to celebrate the historic victory of Barack Hussein Obama, the first African American to be elected president of the United States of America.

As the newly elected president made his appearance to deliver his victory speech, the crowd became almost overwhelmed with joy and excitement. Tears rolled down the cheeks of some. Others held signs that read "Yes, We Can!" Millions more across the nation and around the world joined the celebration as they watched it on television. There was much to celebrate. The United States had reached another major milestone in its more than 200 years as a nation. Overcoming seemingly insurmountable odds to outdistance his opponent, Senator John McClain, Barack Obama broke down a barrier that many thought would take several more generations to accomplish. On November 5, 2012, President Obama was elected to a second term to the highest office in the land.

Barack was born in Honolulu, HI. His mother, Stanley Ann Durham, was a white Kansan and his father, Barack Obama, Sr., was a student from Kenya. The couple separated when Barack, Sr. went to Harvard on a scholarship. They divorced in 1964.

Later Barack's mother married Lolo Soetoro, an Indonesian and the family moved to Indonesia. From age six to ten, Barack attended local schools in Indonesia. In 1971, he moved to Honolulu to live with his maternal grandparents. Following his graduation from high school, Barack attended Occidental College in Los Angeles. After two years, he transferred to Columbia University in New York City where he received a bachelor's degree in 1981.

Barack worked in New York following graduation and later became a director of the Developing Communities Project (DCP), a church-based community organization that helped poor and working class citizens of Chicago. Believing he would be better equipped to help the poor if he were a lawyer, in 1988, he entered Harvard Law School where he was selected as an editor of the *Harvard Law Review* at the end of his first year, and president of the journal in his second year. After receiving his law degree, he accepted a two-year position as Visiting Law and Government Fellow at the University of Chicago Law School. He then served as a professor at the Chicago Law School for 12 years. Throughout these years, Barack kept his commitment to help the poor and working class people of Chicago, serving on the boards of a number of community organizations.

In 1997, Barack turned to politics as a way to help others. He was elected to the Illinois Senate for three terms from 1997 to 2004 and in 2004 he was elected to the U.S. Senate. During the 2004 Democratic Convention, Barack gave a speech that electrified the delegates and the millions of Americans who had tuned in to watch. That speech gave him national exposure.

On February 10, 2007, in Springfield, IL, Barack Obama announced his candidacy for president of the United States. Very few citizens gave the young, energetic candidate a chance to win the Democratic nomination for president against political stalwarts such as Hillary Clinton, John Edwards, and Bill Richardson. But Barack secured the victory and ran a successful campaign to defeat the Republican candidate and claim the highest political office in the land.

Barack Obama overcame many obstacles in his life. But he was always deter-

Democratic presidential nominee Barack Obama and his family, with vice-presidential nominee Joseph Biden and his wife Jill, at the 2008 Democratic Convention following the Obama acceptance speech.

" IN HIS OWN WORDS "

We have been told we cannot do this by a chorus of cynics who will only grow louder and more dissonant in the weeks to come. We've been asked to pause for a reality check. We've been warned against offering the people of this nation false hope. But in the unlikely story that is America, there has never been anything false about hope. For when we have faced down impossible odds; when we've been told that we're not ready, or that we shouldn't try or that we can't, generations of Americans have responded with a simple creed that sums up the spirit of a people. 'Yes we can.'   —from Barack Obama's speech following the New Hampshire Primary, January 8, 2008

OWENS, JESSE
1913 – 1980

birthplace—Danville, AL

"A Blaze of Glory"

The 1936 Olympic games that were held in Germany were about more than just sports. Adolph Hitler, the Nazi leader, said that Germans were a "master race." Many Germans believed him. They thought that Germany should rule the world. Hitler and his followers were sure that the Olympic games would prove they were right. But Jesse Owens had other ideas.

At Ohio State University, Jesse won a record eight individual National Collegiate Athletic Association (NCAA) championships, four each in 1935 and 1936. Despite his athletic success, Jesse never received a scholarship. He had to work part-time to pay for tuition. He even had to live off campus, along with other African-American athletes.

These harsh treatments didn't stop Jesse from being his best on the track. In 1936, he showed the world just what a great athlete he was. In a blaze of glory, he won three gold medals—in the broad jump, the 100-meter dash, and the 200-meter dash, and his speed helped his team win a gold medal in the 440-meter relay. Jesse changed history by setting these new world records.

Adolph Hitler was furious. A black man had embarrassed him before the world. Jesse proved that people are winners because of their talent, not because of their color or nationality. In Berlin, Germany in 1936, the whole world stopped to salute the talents of Jesse Owens.

Did You Know? Despite his historic feat, racial prejudice prevented Jesse from benefitting from his Olympic success. At times he ran races against horses to earn money. "People say that it was degrading for an Olympic champion to run against a horse," he said, "but what was I supposed to do? I had four gold medals, but you can't eat four gold medals." Jesse once said, "Hitler didn't snub me—it was FDR who snubbed me. The president didn't even send me a telegram."

PARKS, ROSA
1913 – 2005

birthplace—Tuskegee, AL

"Mother of the Movement"

R osa's feet ached as she walked to the Cleveland Avenue bus stop. It was 1955 in Montgomery, AL. People were rushing home after a hard day of work.

When the bus arrived, all seats were quickly taken. Some people had to stand. Black people could only sit in the back of the bus. The front section was reserved for whites. Although Rosa sat in the section reserved for black people, the bus driver ordered her and three other black people to give their seats to white people. Rosa refused and she was arrested.

Rosa's refusal to give up her seat helped to start a movement against segregation not only in her hometown of Montgomery, Alabama, but across the South. Her actions that afternoon in Montgomery galvanized the black community to boycott buses in the city until seating restrictions against blacks were removed. A young local minister named Martin Luther King, Jr. was also a part of this historic movement that guaranteed Rosa and Martin a place in history.

Rosa Parks often worked two jobs to help support her family. She always found time, however, to help make Montgomery a better city for her people. She was an active member of the local NAACP. In 1957, she and her husband Raymond moved to Hampton, VA, and later that year relocated to Detroit, MI, where she continued to be active until her death in 2005.

Rosa Parks received many honors for her contributions to the world, including Spingarn Medal (1979), the Presidential Medal of Freedom (1996), the Congressional Gold Medal (1994), and a statue in the U.S. Capitol's National Statuary Hall.

Did You Know? In addition to Dr. Martin Luther King, Jr. and Rosa Parks, many others took courageous stands during the civil rights movement. Joanne Robinson was one of these activists. Jeopardizing her position as a teacher at Alabama State College, Joanne and her Woman's Political Council first organized the Montgomery, AL bus boycott.

POWELL, ADAM CLAYTON
1908 – 1972

birthplace—New Haven, CT

"Keep the Faith"

Adam was a child when he first learned the power of words. It was a lesson he never forgot. His father, Adam Clayton Powell, Sr., was an important minister in Harlem, the largest black community in the United States. He often spoke about the injustices that many black Americans faced.

When Adam grew up, he decided to become a minister like his father had been. He was chosen to pastor his father's church, the Abyssinian Baptist Church.

Adam knew that the injustices he fought in New York City could be found elsewhere in America. So he decided to run for Congress and fight for justice for all Americans. He won his first election in 1944.

Adam accomplished many things in Congress. He helped to raise the minimum wage and was one of the strongest supporters of education. He fought to keep the government from spending money on projects that discriminated against black people. Adam became chairman of the very important House Committee on Education and Labor in 1961.

In 1967, Adam was accused of misusing public funds. He was stripped of his seat in Congress. But the man who had urged black Americans to "keep the faith" did not give up. The people of Harlem elected him again in 1969, and public pressure helped him regain back his seat.

Did You Know? African Americans began serving in the U.S. Congress following the American Civil War during a period called Reconstruction. In 1870, Hiram Rhodes Revels (Mississippi senator) and Joseph Rainey (South Carolina representative) were the first African Americans elected to the U.S. Congress.

Q

QUARLES, BENJAMIN
1904 – 1996

birthplace—Boston, MA

"Great Historian"

To prove that he was not a slave, a free Negro had to carry around with him a certificate of freedom. Numbered, registered, and issued by the courts, these "free papers" gave the name, stature, and complexion of the Negro and indicated how his freedom had been obtained. Free papers had to be renewed periodically, for which a fee was assessed.
— from The Negro in the Making of America

When Benjamin was growing up in Boston, MA, there were few books about black history. So when he became a man, he decided to write books that told about the many important contributions that black people had made to American society.

In his research, Benjamin found that black people had played many important roles in American history, but most books did not include these achievements. He knew it was up to him to fill in the missing facts. Benjamin wrote about how black people fought for victory in the Revolutionary War and the Civil War. He also wrote about historic figures such as Frederick Douglass and Abraham Lincoln. He authored a dozen books and countless articles, and served as a professor at Morgan State University in Baltimore, MD, for 40 years.

The historical research Benjamin and other black historians conducted helped all Americans appreciate black contributions and earned Benjamin a place in history as one of the foremost authorities on Black history.

Did You Know? In 1926, historian Carter G. Woodson started "Negro History Week" because African-American contributions "were overlooked, ignored, and even suppressed." Today, Black History Month covers the entire month of February. Other African-Americans historians who have made major contributions through their research and study include Lerone Bennett, Jr., John Hendrik Clark, W.E.B. DuBois, John Hope Franklin, J.A. Rogers, Charles H. Wesley, and Chancellor Williams.

R

ROBESON, PAUL
1898 – 1976

birthplace—Princeton, NJ

"A Man for All Seasons"

A s Paul Robeson walked to the stage, the audience rose to its feet with applause. It was their way of saying, "Welcome home, we love you." The year was 1963. Paul had recently returned to the United States after living in Europe for five years. These people had come to show how much they appreciated him.

Paul was a singer, actor, scholar, lawyer, humanitarian, and athlete. He spoke several languages. There weren't many things he couldn't do.

He graduated from Rutgers University with honors and was selected as an All-American football player. He began his acting career in 1921 at the Harlem YMCA. A year later, his talent was recognized in the play *Emperor Jones*. In a few years, Paul was known around the world as a great singer and actor. His rich baritone voice brought joy to millions.

Paul knew many people would listen to him because he was famous. So he spoke out against the racism and injustice he saw in America and the world. Some people tried to silence him. In 1950, the U.S. government took away his passport. He couldn't perform in other countries, and concert halls in America were closed to him. He was unable to earn a living doing what he loved most. But Paul still spoke out. When the government was forced to give back his passport in 1958, he went to England. He didn't return until 1963.

Despite the many attempts to discredit him, people around the world continued to love and respect Paul Robeson. He will always be remembered as an outstanding entertainer and humanitarian who made great sacrifices to help his fellow man.

" IN HIS OWN WORDS "

Just a moment. This is something that I challenge very deeply, and very sincerely: that the success of a few Negroes, including myself or Jackie Robinson can make up—and here is a study from Columbia University—for seven hundred dollars a year for thousands of Negro families in the South. My father was a slave, and I have cousins who are sharecroppers, and I do not see my success in terms of myself. That is the reason my own success has not meant what it should mean: I have sacrificed literally hundreds of thousands, if not millions, of dollars for what I believe in.   —from Paul Robeson's testimony before the House Committee on Un-American Activities, June 12, 1956

ROBINSON, JACKIE ROOSEVELT
1919 – 1972

birthplace—Cairo, GA

"He Had the Right Stuff"

For decades, Major League Baseball in the United States was segregated. But in 1947, a courageous and exceptional athlete named Jackie Roosevelt Robinson put an end to this horrible practice.

He had to endure racial taunts and even physical abuse from white fans and white opponents. His play on the field had to be superb. Jackie not only met those expectations, he exceeded them. And because he did so, he made it possible for other African Americans and men of color to play Major League Baseball.

Jackie was born in Cairo, GA, but his family moved to Pasadena, CA, when he was young. His athletic talents were evident at an early age. In high school, he excelled in football, baseball, track, and tennis. He continued his athletic successes at Pasadena Junior College and at UCLA in Los Angeles, CA.

In 1942, he was drafted into the Army, which was also segregated. Jackie earned the rank of second lieutenant, but his army career was cut short when he was court-martialed because he objected to an incident of racial discrimination. He left the Army in 1944, but with an honorable discharge.

In 1945, Jackie was signed to a contract by Branch Rickey of the Brooklyn Dodgers. He spent a season with Montreal, a Dodgers' minor league team. Then, on April 15, 1947, Jackie made his major league debut at Ebbets Field in Brooklyn, NY, before a crowd of 26,623 spectators, including more than 14,000 black fans. Although he failed to get a base hit, on that day, Jackie Roosevelt Robinson became the first black player since the 1880s to play Major League Baseball.

Did You Know? In more than ten seasons with the Brooklyn Dodgers, Jackie Robinson played in six World Series and was selected to play in six consecutive All-Star Games. He was the recipient of the inaugural MLB Rookie of the Year Award in 1947, and won the National League Most Valuable Player Award in 1949—the first black player so honored. He was inducted into the Baseball Hall of Fame, the sports' highest honor, in 1962. In 1997, Major League Baseball retired his uniform number, 42, across all major league teams.

RUDOLPH, WILMA
1940 – 1994

birthplace—Clarksville, TN

"A Golden Track Star"

Wilma never liked to lose. She always tried very hard to be a winner—and her determined spirit usually led to success.

Wilma, the 20th of 22 other brothers and sisters, was born prematurely. Then, she was crippled by polio. She recovered, but her left leg and foot were badly twisted. Her family drove her regularly from her home to Nashville, TN for treatments to straighten her twisted leg. Wilma wore a leg brace for three years. By the time she was 12 years old, she had also survived scarlet fever, whooping cough, chicken pox, and measles.

But Wilma was determined. She not only overcame those illnesses and learned to walk again, she became an outstanding athlete.

In high school, Wilma won many races. She was also a star basketball player. In 1956, she scored 803 points during one season. Her athletic talent earned her a track scholarship to Tennessee State University where she graduated in 1963. While competing in the 1960 Olympic games held in Rome, Wilma became the first woman to win three Olympic medals in track. She was recognized as the world's fastest woman runner.

The 1960 Olympics was the first one to receive international television coverage. So Wilma's feat helped to elevate women's track to a major presence in the United States and around the world. Her blazing speed earned her the nickname, "The Tornado." The French called her "The Black Pearl." In 1960, the Associated Press voted her female athlete of the year.

Wilma went on to become a teacher, coach, and sports commentator. Her winning spirit still inspires athletes today.

Did You Know? In 1904, in St. Louis, MO, George Poage became the first African American to compete and win a medal in the Olympic games. He won a bronze medal in both the 200- and 400-meter hurdles. John Taylor was the first black runner to win a gold medal as a member of the 1908 men's medley relay team. In 1948, Alice Coachman won the high jump competition in London, becoming the first African-American woman to win a gold medal at the Olympic games.

SIRLEAF, ELLEN JOHNSON
1938 –

birthplace—Monrovia, Liberia

"A Trailblazer in Africa"

Ellen Johnson Sirleaf is the only woman to head a country in Africa. She was elected the 24th president of Liberia in 2005 and took office in January 2006.

Ellen was born in Liberia, but she was educated in the United States. She attended the University of Wisconsin and Harvard University. After returning to Liberia in 1979, she began a career in government, serving as assistant minister of finance and then as minister of finance from 1979 to 1980 under President William Tolbert.

In 1980, President Tolbert was assassinated during a coup led by Samuel Doe. Ellen narrowly escaped and fled to Kenya. For the next 20 years, the country of Liberia was in political turmoil. Samuel Doe was assassinated in 1990 during a coup led by Charles Taylor. During this period, Ellen had to live abroad in fear for her life. First, she lived in Nairobi, Kenya, and then she moved to the United States. But she never gave up hope of going back to her country to help her people. In 1997, she ran for president but lost to Charles Taylor in what some observers called a rigged election.

After Charles Taylor was forced to step down in 2003, Ellen was selected to head the Governance Reform Commission, which was responsible for helping to set up elections in the country. In 2005, she ran for the highest office in the land and was victorious.

Did You Know? In 1822, Liberia was established by the American Colonization Society as a place to send former African-American slaves as well as free blacks. Many of those who supported this movement, most of whom were white, believed sending blacks to Liberia was preferable to emancipation. On July 26, 1847, black American settlers declared the independence of the Republic of Liberia.

SMITH, BESSIE
1894 – 1937

birthplace—Chattanooga, TN

"Empress of the Blues"

When Bessie was young, Ma Rainey, the first of the great Blues singers, took Bessie under her wing and helped her find a job. Blues is very special music, and not everyone can sing it well. Ma Rainey knew a good Blues singer when she heard one. She was sure that the young singer would become great.

Bessie's mother and father died when she was young. She and her siblings were raised by Viola, their older sister. To earn money to help the family, Bessie and her brother Andrew performed on street corners in Chattanooga, TN, their home town. Bessie sang and her brother danced. That was Bessie's beginning as an entertainer. She went on to become the highest-paid black entertainer of her day, heading her own shows, which sometimes featured as many as 40 other performers. She even toured in her own special railroad car.

Bessie sang about things in life that give people "the blues"—poverty, racism, and love that is not returned. Her strong, beautiful voice was so powerful, she didn't need a microphone. Her songs captured the sadness and joy of many black Americans.

Bessie sang in many clubs and small southern theaters. In 1923, she went to New York to make her first record. Many recordings followed. "Down Hearted Blues" sold more than two million copies.

Many people who heard Bessie sing believed that "the Empress" was one of the greatest Blues singers who ever lived.

Did You Know?	Blues emerged from black communities in the Deep South during the end of the 19th century. When African Americans migrated to large cities like Chicago in the 1920s, they took this music with them. Hart Wand and W.C. Handy were the first to publish Blues sheet music in 1912. The first recording by an African American singer was "Crazy Blues," performed by Mamie Smith, released in 1920. Called the "Father of the Blues," W. C. Handy was a formally trained musician, composer, and arranger who helped to popularize the Blues during its early years.

STILL, WILLIAM GRANT
1895 – 1978

birthplace—Woodville, MS

"The Dean of Black Composers"

William loved music. He could create songs, but he wanted others to be able to play and enjoy them. He knew he must learn how to write down his music.

For many years, some people thought that black musicians could not play so-called serious music. They believed that music by black composers was not important enough to write down. William knew they were wrong.

He attended the Oberlin Conservatory of Music and the New England Conservatory of Music. He studied very hard and learned how to compose. He created symphonies, operas, ballet music, and musical poems. William successfully combined black and European musical traditions. His beautiful compositions were enjoyed by many people.

William was determined to show that black conductors could lead orchestras as well as white conductors. In 1936, he became the first black person to conduct a major orchestra in the United States when he led the Los Angeles Philharmonic Orchestra. In 1955, he led the New Orleans Philharmonic Orchestra, becoming the first black person to lead an orchestra in the Deep South. During his illustrious career, William wrote eight operas, arranged music for films such as *Pennies from Heaven* starring Bing Crosby, *Lost Horizon* starring Ronald Colman and Jane Wyatt, and arranged music for television and radio shows.

Did You Know? Florence Beatrice Smith Price was the first black woman composer to have a symphonic composition performed by a major American symphony orchestra. The Chicago Symphony Orchestra performed her "Symphony in E Minor" on June 15, 1933. Considered the first black woman in the United States to be recognized as a symphonic composer, Florence composed more than 300 works during her lifetime. An elementary school in Chicago is named in her honor.

T

TRUTH, SOJOURNER
1797 – 1883

birthplace—Hurley, NY

"Freedom's Messenger"

Sojourner was born a slave named Isabella Baumfree. New York, the state where she lived, outlawed slavery in 1827. But Sojourner's master didn't care. He would not free her. So she ran away.

When Sojourner was 46 years old, she decided to start her own campaign against slavery. She could not stand to see her people suffer any longer. She changed her name to Sojourner Truth. She chose that name because she planned to travel from place to place telling the truth about slavery.

Sojourner carried her anti-slavery message throughout the North. She spoke to anyone who would listen—and to those who wouldn't, too. She was a great speaker. Some people compared her to Frederick Douglass.

Sojourner was often beaten for speaking out against slavery. But this brave woman could not be stopped. She had a mission.

After the North's victory in the Civil War in 1865, the passage of the Thirteenth Amendment ended slavery in the United States. But racial discrimination and prejudice against African Americans continued. So Sojourner continued to fight for black equality and for women's rights. She dedicated her life to opening the doors of freedom for all people.

" IN HER OWN WORDS "

That man over there says that women need to be helped into carriages, and lifted over ditches, and to have the best place everywhere. Nobody ever helps me into carriages, or over mud-puddles, or gives me any best place! And ain't I a woman? Look at me! Look at my arm! I have ploughed and planted, and gathered into barns, and no man could head me! And ain't I a woman? I could work as much and eat as much as a man—when I could get it and bear the lash as well! And ain't I a woman? I have borne thirteen children, and seen most all sold off to slavery, and when I cried out with my mother's grief, none but Jesus heard me! And ain't I a woman?

—Sojourner Truth, from a speech delivered at the Women's Rights Convention, Akron, OH, 1851

TUBMAN, HARRIET
c. 1820 – 1913

birthplace—Dorcester County, MD

"Black Moses"

The small band of runaway slaves hid behind trees. They huddled together to hide from the cruel slave catchers. Would the runaways be caught and taken back to slavery? Or would they escape to freedom in the North?

"Not a sound from anyone!" a voice warned. It was Harriet Tubman. She knew the risks and dangers they all faced. This trip to lead slaves from the South was not her first.

Soon the slave catchers were gone. The group of runaway slaves traveled through the dark woods and escaped to the North. "Black Moses" had struck again.

Harriet Tubman led more than 300 slaves to freedom. Although Harriet had escaped from slavery, she made many dangerous trips back to help others find the road to freedom. She used an established route called the Underground Railroad. Along this route, friends and supporters provided safe hiding places, food, and clothing for the runaway slaves.

Angry slave owners offered huge rewards for Harriet's capture, but she managed to fool them again and again. As a "conductor" on the Underground Railroad, Harriet Tubman never lost a passenger.

After the Civil War, Harriett retired to her home in Auburn, NY, where she cared for her aging parents and became active in the women's suffrage movement.

Did You Know?
In 1908, Harriet Tubman established a home for the elderly in Auburn, NY, located next to her own home. She used her own life savings to finance it. Both her home and the home for the aged were designated National Historic Landmarks. In 2004, a $110-million National Underground Railroad Freedom Center opened in Cincinnati, OH, to commemorate the efforts of Harriet Tubman and others who helped overcome slavery and other barriers to freedom. Tubman's stories and the stories of other freedom fighters are highlighted on a Teaching Personal Freedom Tour at the center.

U

UGGAMS, LESLIE
1943 –

birthplace—New York, NY

"A Young Star"

Leslie sang almost from the time she could talk. When she was six years old, she made her singing debut. A short while later she appeared in the television series *Beulah*, starring Ethel Waters.

In 1961, Leslie became a cast member on the popular program *Sing Along With Mitch*. In a short time, her charming voice and perky style attracted fans everywhere. She was a star at only 18 years old. For several years, she was the only black entertainer to be seen regularly on television. In 1969, *The Leslie Uggams Show*, starring Leslie, premiered on CBS television. It was the first variety show with an African-American host to feature a large number of blacks in the cast. It also featured a series of sketches called "Sugar Hill," which dealt with the lives of a middle-class black family in a large American city.

Leslie is not only a singer, but also an actress. She starred in the award-winning television movie *Roots*, which was based upon the book of the same name. This story details the history of a black family from its beginning in Africa to present-day America. Leslie is still performing today.

Did You Know?	African-American Television Firsts
	• Ethel Waters became the first star of a network television sitcom, *Beulah*, (1950).
	• Nat King Cole became the first star of a network television show, *Nat King Cole Show* (1956).
	• Louis Loman became the first African-American television journalist (1959).
	• Cicely Tyson became the first actress to appear as a regular on a dramatic television feature, "East Side/West Side" (1963).
	• Bill Cosby became the first star of a network television drama, *I Spy* (1965).
	• Max Robinson became the first network news anchor (1978).
	• Esther Rolle was first to win an Emmy Award for *Summer of My German Soldier* (1979).

Slaves plan a revolt.

VESEY, DENMARK
1767 – 1822

birthplace—Haiti

"Lover of Freedom"

Denmark Vesey stared out at the angry crowd of whites who were waiting to see him hanged. But he was not afraid. It didn't matter what they thought. He was willing to die for freedom.

It was summer in Charleston, SC, the city where Denmark lived, and slavery was an important part of life in America. Although Denmark had bought his freedom with money he won in a lottery, he could not buy his children's freedom.

Denmark became a dedicated fighter against slavery. He believed black people were being held illegally. To free slaves in the Charleston area, he planned an uprising. He recruited allies and drew up a battle plan. He planned to take over the city on the second Sunday in July of 1822. But his plan was discovered. Denmark and some of his followers were arrested and sentenced to be hanged. Although he did not succeed, Denmark's efforts focused attention on the struggle to end slavery.

Abolitionists viewed Denmark as a hero. Frederick Douglass used his name as a rallying cry to the 54th Massachusetts Volunteer Infantry, one of the first official black units in the Union army during the Civil War. Denmark's rebellion, however, caused panic among whites in Charleston and across the South.

It was quiet now. The crowd moved away. The man who just wanted to see his people free was dead. It seemed strange that two days later, on July 4th, the country celebrated its own freedom.

Did You Know?	Numerous rebellions and insurrections took place during the years that slavery was practiced in the United States. More than 250 uprisings or attempted uprisings involving ten or more people have been documented. The best-known revolts were by Gabriel Prosser in Virginia in 1800, Denmark Vesey in 1822, and Nat Turner in Virginia in 1831. These uprisings as well as other tactics proved that African Americans were not content and happy with their enslaved status.

W

WASHINGTON, BOOKER T.
1856 – 1915

birthplace—Franklin County, VA

"A Great Leader"

Booker was a small boy when slavery ended. He worked in the salt mines of West Virginia from four in the morning until late at night to earn enough money for food. Booker was convinced that education was the key to success. He was determined to learn. He studied by the light of the fire each night after he came home from work.

When he was 15, Booker left home and entered Hampton Institute. He cleaned buildings and classrooms to pay his college tuition. He wanted to become a teacher. After attending Wayland Seminary, Booker taught school in West Virginia.

In 1881, Booker's work as an educator grew when he was chosen to head a newly established school for black students called Tuskegee Normal and Industrial Institute. There were two small, wooden buildings and 30 students when he arrived. Under his leadership, Tuskegee expanded, becoming one of the most important schools for black students in the United States.

Booker became a leader of his people, too. He believed that black Americans should learn trades to improve their economic position. He felt this should be done, even before fighting for integration and equality. Some people disagreed with him, especially William E.B. DuBois. But Booker continued to fight for equality in his own way, taking his message to influential institutions and to the White House.

Booker T. Washington was born in a slave cabin. But he became one of the most powerful black Americans of his time.

Did You Know? Booker T. Washington encouraged African Americans to focus on economic progress rather than social and political advancement. In a speech delivered at the Atlanta Exposition in 1895, he said, "The opportunity to earn a dollar in a factory just now is worth infinitely more than the opportunity to spend a dollar in an opera house." African American leaders such as W.E.B. DuBois disagreed with Booker. They felt African Americans had to pursue a political and social agenda for equality in addition to an economic one.

WATERS, ETHEL
1896 – 1977

birthplace—Chester, PA

**"An Actress with
a Golden Voice"**

When Ethel was a little girl, her family was so poor she stole food so she would have something to eat. She married when she was 13, but soon left her abusive husband and found work as a maid. She worked for less than five dollars a day. But Ethel never lost hope. She was sure that someday her life would change. She knew that she was talented and she believed in herself. On her 17th birthday, she attended a party at a club in Baltimore, MD, where she was living. She was persuaded to sing two songs, and impressed the audience so much that she was offered professional work at the Lincoln Theatre in Baltimore. That's how her career in music began.

Ethel had a beautiful voice. She could sing Jazz and the Blues. Her singing style made ordinary songs sound very special. Many people came to hear her sing, and she became famous. But she wanted to do more.

She began to act in plays and movies. People who thought she was a great singer now knew that she was a great actress, too. Ethel's beautiful voice and dramatic talent established her as one of the most important actresses of her time.

In 1950, Ethel won the New York Drama Critics Award for her performance in the Broadway play *A Member of the Wedding*, and became the first black to star in a network sitcom, *Beulah*.

Did You Know? Hattie McDaniel (1895–1952) was the most successful black film actor of the 1930s and 1940s. Because of racial prejudice and discrimination, African Americans were relegated to stereotypical roles as maids and domestics. As McDaniel grew more successful, the maids she played became more sassy, independent-minded, and self-assured. Some estimate that she appeared in more than 300 films during her career.

WELLS, IDA B.
1869 – 1931

birthplace—Holly Springs, MS

"A Warrior with Words"

Ida B. Wells' parents were strong people who were born slaves. By example, they taught Ida courage and strength. They also taught her to love freedom as much as they did.

Ida's parents died of yellow fever when she was 16 years old. After their death, she worked as a teacher and helped to raise her seven brothers and sisters. But Ida never forgot her parents' example of courage and strength. For more than 40 years, Ida was one of the most fearless, articulate and respected women in the United States.

After the Civil War ended, new constitutional amendments were passed to end slavery, grant citizenship to African Americans, and give them the right to vote. Quickly, however, towns, cities, and states across the country, especially in the South, began enacting their own laws to deny rights to African Americans. These laws were called "Jim Crow" laws. Cruel and often brutal methods were used to enforce them. These cruelties made Ida angry and she set out to do something about them.

Ida wrote about the many injustices she saw. She made people aware of how black people were suffering. In 1889, she became co-owner and editor of *Free Speech and Headlight*, a newspaper she used to fight against "Jim Crow." In 1894, she published *The Red Record*, the first book to document the lynching of black Americans. Ida was also a founder of the NAACP, was active in the women's suffrage movement, and established several notable organizations, including the Women's Era Club, the first civic organization for black women.

Ida became known in the United States and throughout the world as a fighter for justice.

Did You Know? In 1884, as editor of *Free Speech and Headlight*, a small newspaper published in Memphis, TN, Ida B. Wells wrote about the lynching of black men and women in the South. Then, in 1892, after three African-American businessmen were killed in Memphis, she wrote an article urging African Americans to leave Memphis. Many did. Wells had to leave also because she feared for her life.

WHEATLEY, PHILLIS
1753 – 1784

birthplace—Senegal, West Africa

"A Poet for Her Times"

The goddess comes, she moves divinely fair,
Olive and laurel bind her golden hair:
Wherever shines this native of the skies,
Unnumber'd charms and recent graces rise.

— from "To His Excellency, General Washington"

Phillis was very young when she was stolen from her parents and brought to America. She would never forget her parents, her African homeland, or her trip on the horrible slave ship. She was bought by the Wheatleys, a family of white merchants. As their slave, she had to do whatever they asked.

But the Wheatleys soon realized that Phillis was a very special child. They taught her how to read and write. By the time she was 14, she had written her first poem.

Soon many people began to read her poetry. One of her poems, which was dedicated to George Washington, brought her much attention. In 1773, Phillis published a collection of poems entitled *Poems on Various Subjects, Religious and Moral.*

Phillis Wheatley was only 31 years old when she died. But she will be remembered as one of America's first black poets.

Did You Know?

Lucy Terry was the author of the oldest known piece of black literature in the United States. Her poem "Bars Fight" was written in 1746, but wasn't published until 1855. Jupiter Hammon (1711–1806) is considered the first published black writer. His poem, "An Evening Thought: Salvation by Christ with Penitential Cries," was published in 1761. Harriet Wilson (1825–1900) and William Wells Brown (1814–1884) wrote two of the first novels published by black Americans. Brown's *Clotel: or The President's Daughter* (1853) was published in England. Wilson's *Our Nig* (1859) was published in the United States.

X, MALCOLM
1925 – 1965

birthplace—Omaha, NE

"Fighter for Freedom"

No one expressed the anger that many black Americans felt during the 1950s and 1960s more vividly than Malcolm X. He lashed out at society's unfair treatment of his people and warned America that black people would no longer accept racial injustice.

Born Malcolm Little, he was only six years old when his father was killed. His mother had a nervous breakdown several years later and Malcolm was sent to live in a foster home.

Malcolm had trouble adjusting to life without his family. Although he was a good student, he dropped out of school at 15. Before he was 21, he was sent to prison for burglary.

In prison, Malcolm discovered a religious group called the Nation of Islam. This organization of black Muslims helped him find a new purpose in life. Malcolm Little became Malcolm X, the leading spokesman for the Nation of Islam. He established its national newspaper and helped to organize bakeries and stores. He was also a powerful speaker. Many black Americans looked to Malcolm as their leader.

Malcolm left the Nation of Islam in 1963 and formed the Organization of Afro-American Unity. Following a trip to Mecca, he changed his name to El Hajj Malik El-Shabazz. His fight for freedom continued.

On February 21, 1965, Malcolm was killed by assassins. But he had already made his mark in the struggle for justice for black Americans.

> ## IN HIS OWN WORDS
>
> We declare our right on this earth to be a human being, to be respected as a human being, to be given the rights of a human being in this society, on this earth, in this day, which we intend to bring into existence by any means necessary.
>
> —variation of speech by El Hajj Malik El-Shabazz at Founding Rally of the Organization of Afro-American Unity,

YOUNG, WHITNEY M., JR.
1921 – 1971

birthplace—Lincoln Ridge, KY

"A Dynamic Leader"

It has become necessary for me to face realistically the true state of America's development as it seeks to make operational, and give honest meaning to, its creed of equal opportunity and justice for all.
                                                                    —from *To Be Equal*

The 1960s were a time of change. Many black people fought for civil rights and equality. Whitney Young, Jr., was one such strong leader who worked hard to make a better life for his people.

At first, Whitney wanted to become a doctor. But he saw many problems in the world that bothered him. He decided that he could do more to help people by becoming a social worker. Eventually he became the dean of Atlanta University's School of Social Work. In 1961, Whitney was appointed head of the National Urban League. This organization was formed in 1910 to help bring educational opportunities and employment to black Americans, especially in the North. He knew that there were many rich people in the United States who could help poor people. He worked to find ways for them to contribute.

Whitney convinced many corporations and foundations to sponsor self-help programs that would help guide black people toward jobs, education, and housing. Through his leadership, many people were given the help they needed to build themselves a better life.

Did You Know?

Whitney Young was a member of the "Big Six," the name given to the leaders of the most prominent civil rights organizations during the 1960s. Others included Dr. Martin Luther King, Jr., Southern Christian Leadership Conference (SCLC); James Farmer, Congress of Racial Equality (CORE); John Lewis, Student Non-Violent Coordinating Committee (SNCC); Roy Wilkins, National Association for the Advancement of Colored People (NAACP); and A. Philip Randolph, Brotherhood of Sleeping Car Porters. All six men played major roles in the historic 1963 March on Washington.

Z

ZULU, SHAKA
1787 – 1828

birthplace—Zulu Kingdom,
South Africa

"A Great General"

The mere mention of Shaka's name made his enemies tremble with fear. He was one of the greatest African generals who ever lived. His army was one of the most fearless in the world.

Shaka was born a Zulu prince, but his father would not claim him as his son. Oral history indicates that he and his mother Nandi wandered from village to village trying to find a home. People called Shaka's mother names, and children threw stones at him. But these hard times made Shaka strong. He had been told that he was destined to rule the Zulus and Shaka never forgot this prophesy. The Mtetwa, powerful rivals of the Zulus, accepted Shaka and his mother into their clan. Over time, Shaka became a great warrior. In the early 1800s, the king of the Mtetwa, ordered Shaka to conquer the Zulus. Shaka was pleased. Now was his chance to claim his birthright. He conquered the Zulus and became their leader. Shaka was also known for exercising great brutality toward his enemies.

Shaka organized his army into a powerful force that conquered many other clans in southern Africa. He used new military techniques and weapons. Under his leadership, the Zulus became the most powerful nation in southern Africa. Numerous legends have grown during modern times from telling and retelling Shaka Zulu's experiences as a warrior and military leader and his final assassination in 1828.

Did You Know? At the time of his death, Shaka ruled over 250,000 people and had more than 50,000 warriors. He ruled the Zulu nation for 10 years. The new airport at La Mercy in Durban, South Africa, built in preparation for the 2010 FIFA World Cup, was named after this African king.

"Hero . . . one noted for feats of courage or nobility of purpose; especially one who has risked or sacrificed his life. A person prominent in some event, field, period, or cause by reason of special achievements or contributions."

—*The American Heritage Dictionary*

THE EMANCIPATION PROCLAMATION
150th ANNIVERSARY

January 1, 2013 marked the 150th Anniversary of the Emancipation Proclamation, which freed slaves in ten states at war with the Union. This landmark executive order was issued by President Abraham Lincoln. President Lincoln acted under what he interpreted as power granted to him by the U.S. Constitution as Commander-in-Chief of the Army and Navy of the United States. It is the responsibility of the U.S. Congress to pass laws, not the president. Why then did President Lincoln take this bold step with which many in the country at that time disagreed?

When the Civil War started in 1861, some in the North thought it would end quickly. The Union had more men and it was better prepared for war. But the South proved to be a stubborn and determined foe. It became obvious after a number of Southern victories, that the war would be lengthy and hard fought, and that Northern success was not assured.

On September 22, 1862, after the Union's victory at Antietam, Lincoln issued a preliminary decree stating that, unless the rebellious states returned to the Union by January 1, freedom would be granted to slaves within those states. The decree also left room for a plan to compensate for emancipation. Lincoln had first shown his cabinet a draft of the decree on July 22, 1862. No Confederate states took the offer. Instead, they remained steadfast in their fight to become an inde-

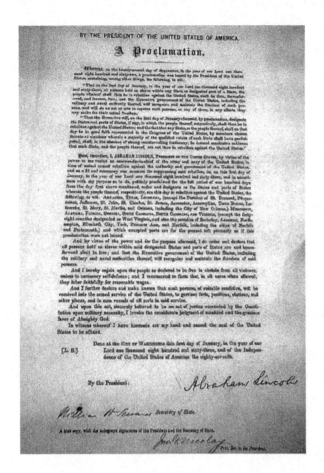

This copy of the Emancipation Proclamation signed by President Abraham Lincoln, is one of 24 known copies to survive out of 48 that were originally printed.

pendent nation. So, on January 1, 1863, the Emancipation Proclamation became law.

Nearly 3.1 million of the 4 million enslaved blacks were held in bondage in the states of the Confederacy. The Proclamation immediately freed 50,000 slaves, with many of the rest of the 3.1 million freed as Union armies advanced in territories held by the South. The Emancipation Proclamation also allowed freed slaves to serve in the Union army. During the war nearly 200,000 blacks, most of them ex-slaves, joined Union forces. Their contributions gave the North additional manpower that was significant in winning the war.

The Proclamation did not compensate slave-owners and did not itself outlaw slavery. Nor did it make the ex-slaves citizens.

Was Lincoln motivated by a moral conviction or was his decree strictly a military policy? Perhaps noted black historian John Hope Franklin explains it best. He wrote, "If the Proclamation of Emancipation was essentially a war measure, it had the desired effect of creating confusion in the South and depriving the Confederacy of much of its valuable laboring force. If it was a diplomatic document, it succeeded in rallying to the Northern cause thousands of English and European laborers who were anxious to see workers gain their freedom throughout the world. If it was a humanitarian document, it gave hope to millions of Negroes that a better day lay ahead, and it renewed the faith of thousands of crusaders who had fought long to win freedom in America."

Lincoln and his cabinet, painted by F. B. Carpenter, engraved by A. H. Ritchie. Courtesy Library of Congress.

"Watch Night," by W. T. Carlton, 1863.

WATCH NIGHT

Watch Night service is a Methodist custom that African Americans adopted and adapted as their own spiritual ritual. Richard Allen, founder of the African Methodist Church, and other Black Methodists, observed Watch Night during the early 1800s. But on December 31, 1862, Watch Night would take on an even more important significance for African Americans. On that night, in cities and towns across the country, blacks, free and enslaved, and abolitionists, gathered in churches, waiting anxiously for confirmation that the Emancipation Proclamation, which would end slavery in ten confederate states, had indeed become law as had been promised. The decree drafted by President Abraham Lincoln would be a major step towards freedom.

Abolitionist and former slave Frederick Douglass stayed at a church in Rochester, NY, until 10 p.m. on New Year's Day, waiting for a cable that would assure him that the law had been passed.

Today, many African American Christians observe Watch Night at church services. Some may not be aware of the link to "Freedom's Eve," December 31, 1862. Others, however, are aware and celebrate it by reading the Emancipation Proclamation and other programs of remembrance. But for all, Watch Night is a way to greet the New Year with jubilation and praise, praying, shouting, and thanking God for allowing them to live and survive another year as they anticipate the fulfillment of their hopes and God's promises in the New Year, just as their ancestors did on "Freedom's Eve."

CHRONOLOGY

1500s The British, Dutch, Spanish, and Portuguese begin trafficking African people in the brutal European slave trade.

1619 The first boatload of Africans arrives in Virginia. Within a few decades, the institution of black slavery is firmly established in the American colonies.

1660 The number of Africans forced into slavery increases rapidly as the British gain control over much of the slave trade.

1770 Phillis Wheatley publishes her first poem, becoming the earliest known published African-American woman writer.

1775 The American Revolution begins. The 13 American colonies fight for their independence from British rule. One of the first casualties of the war is a black man, Crispus Attucks.

1776 Congress adopts the Declaration of Independence and creates the United States of America. Although based on the theory of natural rights, the Declaration of Independence does not extend those rights to African Americans.

1787 The African Free School, the free secular school in New York City, opens.
The Free African Society of Philadelphia, organized by Richard Allen and Absalom Jones, is formed.
The African Grand Lodge is established by Prince Hall.

1783 The Treaty of Paris recognizes the United States as a nation, ending the American Revolution.

1791 Toussaint L'Ouverture leads a successful slave revolt in Haiti. Haiti becomes the first independent black nation in the Western Hemisphere.
Benjamin Banneker becomes the first African American to publish an almanac.

1793 The Fugitive Slave Act is passed. This law makes harboring a slave a criminal offense.

1798 Abolitionist James Forten, Sr., establishes a successful sail-making shop in Philadelphia.

1807 Britain outlaws the slave trade and later abolishes slavery in the British Empire (1833), but American slaveholders continue to keep one million African-American slaves under their control to work the plantations of the Southern states.

1821 The first black theatrical company, the African Grove Theater, is formed in New York City.

1822 Denmark Vesey organizes a slave revolt in Charleston, SC.

1827 *Freedom's Journal*, the first black newspaper in the United States, with John Russwurm and Samuel Cornish serving as editors, is published.

1839 Joseph Cinque and other captured Africans take over the slave ship *Amistad*, demanding to be returned to Africa. They are ultimately set free by a U.S. Supreme Court decision in 1841.

1843 Sojourner Truth starts her own campaign against slavery.
Norbert Rillieux patents his vacuum evaporation system, which revolutionizes the sugar industry and food preparation in general.

1846 Harriet Tubman escapes slavery and begins conducting on the Underground Railroad.

1848 The right of women to vote is proposed for the first time by women's rights leaders Elizabeth Cady Stanton and Lucretia Mott.

1850 The Underground Railroad is fully functioning, helping Southern slaves escape to the North and Canada.

1853 William Wells Brown becomes America's first African-American novelist when his book *Clotel or, the President's Daughter: A Narrative of Slave Life in the United States* is published in England.

CHRONOLOGY

1857 In the Dred Scott decision, the U.S. Supreme Court denies citizenship to blacks, opens federal territory to slavery, and decrees that slaves are not free just because they are taken into free territory.

1861 The Civil War begins between the North and the South. Many slaves flee to the South Carolina Sea Islands. There Charlotte Forten Grimke teaches freedmen how to read and write.

1863 President Abraham Lincoln signs the Emancipation Proclamation, granting freedom to slaves in ten states of the Confederacy.

1864 Rebecca Cole and Rebecca Lee are the first two African-American women in the United States to receive medical degrees.

1865 The Civil War ends with a Northern victory.
Henry Highland Garnet delivers a speech in the hall of the U.S. House of Representatives.
The Thirteenth Amendment, which abolishes slavery in the United States, is enacted.

1868 The Fourteenth Amendment, which provides African Americans protection and privileges of natural citizens and gives them Constitutional guarantees is enacted.

1870 Hiram M. Revels becomes the first African-American U.S. senator when he is elected from the state of Mississippi.
The Fifteenth Amendment, which guarantees the right to vote to all men, is enacted.

1872 Charlotte Ray becomes the first African-American woman to receive a law degree in the United States.
P.B.S. Pinchback of Louisiana becomes the first African American to serve as governor of a state.

1876 Meharry Medical College becomes the first medical school founded for the education of African Americans.

1882 Lewis H. Latimer patents the first cost-efficient method of producing carbon filaments for electric lights.

1883 Jan Matzeliger patents the first successful shoe lasting machine.

1892 Ida B. Wells starts her lifelong anti-lynching campaign by establishing her own newspaper, the *Memphis Free Speech*, to draw attention to the brutal lynch mob murders of black Americans.

1895 Booker T. Washington delivers his Atlanta Compromise speech at the Atlanta Exposition.
Ida B. Wells publishes *The Red Record*, a pamphlet that exposes lynching in America.

1896 Mary Church Terrell is elected president of the National Association of Colored Women.
In *Plessey v. Ferguson*, the U.S. Supreme Court upholds legal segregation.

1897 Andrew J. Beard patents a coupling devise for railroad cars.

1898 Mary Church Terrell delivers a speech to the National American Suffrage Association in Washington, D.C.

1899 Mary Eliza Mahoney is the first African-American woman to graduate from a professional white nursing school.

1900 James Weldon and his brother J. Rosamond Johnson write "Lift Ev'ry Voice and Sing," also known as the black national anthem.

1903 Maggie Lena Walker establishes the St. Luke Penny Savings Bank, which becomes the St. Luke Bank and Trust Company. She becomes America's first woman bank president.

1904 After teaching at Haines Institute (founded by Lucy Craft Laney), Mary McLeod Bethune establishes a school now known as Bethune-Cookman University.

1909 The National Association for the Advancement of Colored People (NAACP) is formed. W.E.B. DuBois, Ida B. Wells, and Mary Church Terrell are founding members.

CHRONOLOGY

1910   Madame C.J. Walker opens her own beauty care factory. She goes on to become America's first black millionaire, a philanthropist, and supporter of black artists in Harlem.

The first case of sickle cell anemia is identified in the United States.

1914   World War I begins. Almost 400,000 African-American men serve in the armed forces, mostly in service units. The 92nd and 93rd all-black infantry divisions, prove to be outstanding fighting forces.

The Universal Negro Improvement Association (UNIA) is formed by Marcus Garvey.

1915   The Great Migration of African Americans from the rural South to northern industrial cities is well underway.

1920   The Nineteenth Amendment to the Constitution guarantees women the right to vote.

1920s   The Harlem Renaissance is at its height. Writers such as Zora Neale Hurston, Arna Bontemps, Jessie Fauset, Claude McKay, Jean Toomer, and Langston Hughes produce some of their greatest works during this period.

1921   Langston Hughes pens his famous poem, "The Negro Speaks of Rivers."

1922   Bessie Coleman, the first black American female pilot, performs in an air show in Chicago.

1923   Garrett A. Morgan patents a three-way automatic traffic signal.

1926   Negro History Week is begun by Carter G. Woodson. It is later expanded to Black History Month.

1929   The Great Depression begins.

1935   The National Council of Negro Women is formed. Mary McLeod Bethune is the founder.

1939   World War II breaks out in Europe. Over one million African Americans serve, including several thousand women. Despite the proven ability of African-American military men, the Armed Forces are still segregated.

1940   *Native Son*, a novel by Richard Wright, is published.

Frederick McKinley Jones patents a practical refrigeration system for trucks and railroad cars.

Dr. Charles Richard Drew is the first person to set up a blood bank.

1941   The United States enters World War II.

1945   World War II ends.

1947   Jackie Robinson becomes the first African American to play Major League Baseball in the modern era when he joins the Brooklyn Dodgers.

1948   Alice Coachman becomes the first African-American woman to win a gold medal in the Olympic games, placing first in the high jump.

The racist system of apartheid is formalized in South Africa.

President Harry S. Truman issues Executive Order 9981, ending segregation in the military.

1950   Attorney Edith Sampson becomes the first African American to serve as a delegate to the United Nations.

For her book of poetry, *Annie Allen*, Gwendolyn Brooks becomes the first African American to win a Pulitzer Prize.

Ralph Bunche is the first African American to win the Nobel Peace Prize.

Earl Lloyd becomes the first African American to play in the National Basketball Association when he suits up for the Washington Capitols. Charles Cooper is the first to be drafted by an NBA team, the Boston Celtics.

1954   In *Brown v. Board of Education* of Topeka, Kansas, the U.S. Supreme Court reverses the "separate but equal" doctrine of *Plessey v. Ferguson* (1896).

CHRONOLOGY

1955   Rosa Parks refuses to give up her seat on a Montgomery, Alabama bus to a white man. The incident sparks a 381-day bus boycott lead by Dr. Martin Luther King, Jr.

1957   Despite threats to their lives, Daisy Bates and the Little Rock Nine successfully integrate Central High School in Little Rock, Arkansas.

Althea Gibson becomes the first African American to win a Wimbledon singles tennis title.

1959   Dr. Martin Luther King, Jr. organizes the Southern Christian Leadership Conference with other black leaders.

Loraine Hansberry's *A Raisin in the Sun* opens on Broadway and wins the New York Drama Critics Circle Award.

1960   Wilma Rudolph becomes the first woman to win three gold medals in track in a single Olympics.

1961   Freedom Rides begin.

1963   The 16th Street Baptist Church in Birmingham, AL, is bombed, killing four black children.

The March on Washington is held.

Civil rights leader Medgar Evers is assassinated in Mississippi.

1964   The Civil Rights Act passes.

1965   The Voting Rights Act of 1965 is passed.

Human rights leader Malcolm X is assassinated.

1968   Dr. Martin Luther King, Jr., is assassinated in Memphis, TN.

Shirley Chisholm is elected the first African-American female congressperson. She is elected from the state of New York.

Arthur Ashe becomes the first African-American male to win a major tennis tournament when he captures the singles title at the United States Lawn Tennis Association Open Tournament.

1972   Shirley Chisholm becomes the first African-American woman to make a bid for the nomination for the presidency of the United States.

In *Roe v. Wade*, the U.S. Supreme Court rules that states may not ban abortions and that the Fourteenth Amendment protects a woman from state intrusion into her decision as to whether or not to bear a child.

1983   Guion Bluford, Jr. becomes the first African American to make a space flight.

January 20 is declared a federal holiday in honor of Dr. Martin Luther King, Jr.

1988   Jesse Jackson becomes the first African American to mount a serious run for the presidency of the United States; he delivers a speech at the National Democratic Convention.

1990   Nelson Mandela is released from prison in South Africa.

1992   Mae C. Jemison becomes the first African-American woman to make a space flight.

1993   Carol Moseley Braun becomes the first African-American woman elected to the U.S. Senate.

Toni Morrison is awarded the Nobel Prize in Literature, "who in novels characterized by visionary force and poetic import, gives life to an essential aspect of American reality."

2001   Colin Powell becomes the first African American to serve as secretary of state.

(Add something about 9/11 attack in NYC, Washington, D.C. etc)

2005   Condoleezza Rice becomes the first African-American woman to serve as secretary of state.

2008   Barack Hussein Obama is the first African American to be elected president of the United States.

2012   Barack Hussein Obama is elected for a second term.

ACKNOWLEDGMENTS

We would like to thank the following people for their valuable assiatance in preparing this book: Wendy Lewison, Carol Drisko, Betty Odabashian, Schomburg Center for Research in Black Culture, New York Public Library, Linda F. McClure, Morgan State University; Katura J. Hudson, Stephan J. Hudson.

Photo Credits

Arista Records: 21

Baseball Hall of Fame: 43

Bettman Newsphotos: 3, 17, 18, 22, 23, 26, 27, 31, 32, 38, 46, 50, cover

Courtesy John Butler: 58

Katherine Dunham Museum, East St. Louis, IL: 13

The DuSable Museum of African American History, Inc., Chicago, IL: 12

Ghanaian Embassy: 35

The Granger Collection: 5

Historical Pictures Service, Chicago, IL: 51

Library of Congress: 61

Monica Morgan: cover photos of Rosa Parks and Barack Obama

Morgan State University, Office of the President: 9

National Portrait Gallery, Smithsonian Institute, Washington, DC: 2, 8, 10, 29, 48, 52, 55, cover

Private Collections:

Schomburg Center for Research in Black Culture, The New York Public Library, Astor, Lenox and Tilden Foundations: 6, 7, 11, 14, 16, 19, 20, 21, 24, 25, 34, 39, 40, 42, 44, 47, 49, 53, 54, 56, 57, cover

Permissions:

p. ii Copyright © 1981 by Houghton Mifflin Company. Adapted and reprinted by permission from *The American Heritage Dictionary of the English Language*.

p. 18 From *To Be Young, Gifted and Black: Lorraine Hansberry in Her Own Words*, adapted by Robert Nemiroff, © 1969. Reprinted by permission of Prentice-Hall, Inc., Englewood Cliffs, NJ.

p. 20 From *Selected Poems of Langston Hughes* by Langston Hughes. © 1959 Reprinted by permission of Alfred Knopf, Inc., New York, NY

p. 21 From *Their Eyes Were Watching God* by Zora Neale Hurston, © 1937, renewed 1965. Reprinted by permission of Harper & Row Publishers Inc., New York, NY.

ABOUT THE AUTHORS

Wade Hudson is the author and editor of 30 books for children and young readers, including *Powerful Words: Two Hundred Years of Extraordinary Writing by African Americans, Jamal's Busy Day* and *Pass It On: African-American Poetry for Children*. He is also co-founder of Just Us Books, Inc. a children's and young adult publishing company and the multicultural imprint, Marimba Books.

Valerie Wilson Wesley writes for children and young adults, as well as having penned novels and mysteries for adult audiences. The popular Tamara Hayle series has gained her a loyal following among mystery fans. Her books for young readers include the *Willimena Rules* series, *Where Do We Go From Here*, a YA novel, and *Freedom's Gifts: A Juneteeth Story*, a picture book.

CPSIA information can be obtained at www.ICGtesting.com
Printed in the USA
LVOW03s1442130815

450005LV00016B/405/P